Family Bible study

THE
Herschel
HOBBS
COMMENTARY

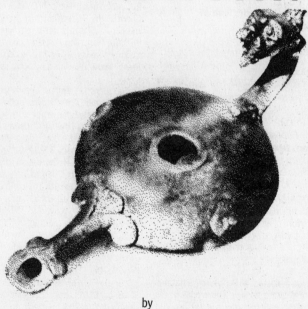

by

Robert J. Dean

FALL 2002
Volume 3, Number 1

GENE MIMS, *President*
LifeWay Church Resources

Ross H. McLaren
Editor-in-Chief

Carolyn Gregory
Copy Editor

Stephen Smith
Graphic Designer

Frankie Churchwell
Technical Specialist

Michael Felder
Lead Adult Ministry Specialist

John McClendon
Mic Morrow
Adult Ministry Specialists

Send questions/comments to
  Editor, *Herschel Hobbs Commentary*
  One LifeWay Plaza
  Nashville, TN 37234-0175
  Or make comments on the web at
  www.lifeway.com

Management Personnel

Louis B. Hanks, *Director*
Publishing
Gary Hauk, *Director*
Adult Ministry Publishing
Bill Craig, *Managing Director*
Adult Ministry Publishing
Alan Raughton, *Director*
Sunday School/Open Group Ministry

The Herschel Hobbs Commentary (ISSN 0191-4219), *Family Bible Study,* is published quarterly for adult teachers and members using the Family Bible Study series by LifeWay Christian Resources of the Southern Baptist Convention, One LifeWay Plaza, Nashville, Tennessee 37234, Gene Mims, President, LifeWay Church Resources, a division of LifeWay Christian Resources; James T. Draper, Jr., President, Ted Warren, Executive Vice-President, LifeWay Christian Resources; Bill L. Taylor, Director, Sunday School Group. © Copyright 2001 LifeWay Christian Resources of the Southern Baptist Convention. All rights reserved. Single subscription to individual address, $20.95 per year. If you need help with an order, WRITE LifeWay Church Resources Customer Service, One LifeWay Plaza, Nashville, Tennessee 37234-0113; For subscriptions, FAX (615) 251-5818 or EMAIL subscribe@lifeway.com. For bulk shipments mailed quarterly to one address, FAX (615) 251-5933 or EMAIL CustomerService@lifeway.com. Order ONLINE at www.lifeway.com. Mail address changes to: *The Herschel Hobbs Commentary, Family Bible Study,* One LifeWay Plaza, Nashville, TN 37234-0113.

Dedicated to

Persecuted Christians,

whose basic human right to worship God

is being denied as they suffer affliction for the sake of Jesus.

Contents

Study Theme

God of Grace and Glory — 6

Study Theme

Covenants of Grace — 56

Contents

Study Theme

Entering into a Covenant of Grace with God   **97**

Study Theme

God of Grace and Glory

Have you ever been a patient in a hospital that trains doctors? If so, you probably have had this experience. A group surrounds your bed. Many are young adults in white coats. Your doctor or another physician describes your symptoms to the group. This is a necessary step in training physicians, but sometimes the patient feels uncomfortable. Some physicians are skilled at involving the patient in this process. Others proceed as if the patient were not there. At those times the patient wants to say: "Hey, that's me you're talking about. Here I am. Talk to me."

I wonder if God sometimes feels that way when we analyze Him in Bible studies and doctrinal discussions. Studying about God—His attributes and His actions—is necessary, but we need to remember to bring Him into the conversation. Let Him speak to us through His Word, as we speak to Him through prayer and praise.

In this five-session study, we will be looking at the "God of Grace and Glory." We will have lessons on God's attributes of holiness, justice, and patience and on His actions in forgiving and in providing. The Bible passages provide a variety of ways to hear God and to speak to Him. The first lesson is based on verses from a psalm in which David called on people to praise the Lord. The second lesson is Ezekiel's quotation of God's words about human accountability and divine justice. The third lesson contains verses from Jonah; some are narrative and some include dialogue between Jonah and God. The fourth lesson is from Psalm 51, David's confession of his sins to the Lord. The fifth lesson is based on the narrative of how God provided for Elijah, but it also includes dialogue between God and Elijah. These are models of various ways of dealing with studying about God. We seek to learn who He is and what He does. We allow Him to speak to us and we speak to Him.

Week of September 1

GOD IS HOLY

Background Passage: 1 Chronicles 15:1–16:43
Focal Passage: 1 Chronicles 16:7-12,15-17,25-29,34-35
Key Verse: 1 Chronicles 16:29

❖ *Significance of the Lesson*

• The *Theme* of this lesson is that God is holy; He is the one true, living God.
• The *Life Question* this lesson seeks to address is, What does it mean that God is holy?
• The *Biblical Truth* is that God's holiness is evident in that He is incomparably great, eternally faithful, exclusively God, and our only Savior.
• The *Life Impact* is to help you worship the holy God.

Reverence for the Holy God

The secular worldview by definition has no interest in God. *Secular* means "of this world" and "nonreligious." Some secular people declare their unbelief in God; most simply live as if God is not a factor in their lives. God is unimportant to them.

The biblical worldview is founded on the reality of God and reverence for Him. God is great and good. He is holy, and people of biblical faith worship and serve Him in reverence and truth. True worship is offered to God Himself.

Word Study: *holy, holiness*

The Hebrew word *qodesh* appears many times in the Old Testament. The basic meaning of the related verb is "to set apart." The noun is "apartness." The adjective is "set apart." Most Old Testament occurrences of this word refer to God. As used for God, the basic meaning is that God is set apart from the rest of His creation. He is the One who is wholly other than human beings. The moral connotation of this word is not apparent in this basic use, however. The word *qodesh* also came to refer to God as righteous, just, good, pure, and so forth. Humans are to respond to God as the wholly other with awe and wonder. We are to respond to Him as morally holy by being holy as He is holy. The wonderful truth of the Bible is that the holy, unapproachable God loves people and offers mercy and grace whereby humans can worship and serve Him.

❖ *Search the Scriptures*

After the ark of the covenant was brought to Jerusalem, David assigned Asaph and his helpers to lead in singing. The song recorded in this passage expresses gratitude and praise to the holy God. It calls people to seek the Lord's presence continually. It recalls God's promises to the patriarchs. The song points to God as the only true God. It calls on the great and good God for salvation. We will look at four aspects of what it means to call God *holy*.

Incomparably Great (1 Chron. 16:7-12)

What was the historical setting? Who was Asaph? What three aspects of worship are in verse 8? What role does music play in worship? How can we magnify God's holy name? How can we seek the Lord's face continually? What lasting truths do these verses reveal about worship?

Verse 7: Then on that day David delivered first this psalm to thank the LORD into the hand of Asaph and his brethren.

The historical setting for this passage is in 1 Chronicles 15:1–16:6. The ark of the covenant had been successfully brought to Jerusalem, and David was encouraging the people to make appropriate responses. The ark was placed in a tent and sacrifices were offered. David gave gifts of food to the people. He appointed some Levites to serve before the ark of the covenant by leading in thanks and praise. The chief of these Levites was a man named Asaph. Others assisted him, and Asaph played the cymbals (v. 5).

Verse 7 tells how **David delivered first this psalm to thank the LORD.** Your Bible probably has the words **this psalm** in italics. This shows that the words are not in the Hebrew text but were added by the translators. The *New International Version* also has the same words. The meaning is that David had written a psalm, which he gave to **Asaph and his brethren.** According to this translation, David was the author and the others sang and played the music for the psalm.

Because the words **this psalm** are not in the Hebrew text, some translations do not make clear who composed the psalm, although all agree that it was used by Asaph and his helpers. For example, the *New American Standard Bible* reads, "Then on that day David first assigned Asaph and his relatives to give thanks to the LORD" (see also NRSV). The meaning of this is that David first appointed Asaph and the others to have charge of the music of the temple. J. A. Thompson, writing in *The New American Commentary,* noted: "The NIV [and thus KJV] suggests that the psalm which follows was given by David to Asaph, but the Hebrew does not say that a psalm was given, only that the act of 'giving thanks' was placed into the hand *(beyad)* of Asaph."[1] This leaves open the question of who wrote the psalm. We know that David wrote many of them, but Asaph also wrote some of the psalms.

Asaph served during the time of David, but a number of his descendants had the same name. Some of the "sons of Asaph," for example, are mentioned in 2 Chronicles 20:14. Psalms 50 and 73-83 are attributed to someone with the same name. We know that the first person by that name mentioned in the Bible was appointed by David to lead music in connection with the ark: "So he left there before the ark of the covenant of the LORD Asaph and his brethren, to minister before the ark continually, as every day's work required" (1 Chron. 16:37). One lasting lesson about worship is that some people are gifted and called to lead in parts of public worship.

Some of the words of the psalm in 1 Chronicles 16:8-36 are found in three other psalms. Verses 8-22 are in Psalm 105:1-15; verses 23-33 are in Psalm 96:1-13; verses 34-36 are in Psalm 106:1,47-48.

Verses 8-12: **Give thanks unto the LORD, call upon his name, make known his deeds among the people. [9]Sing unto him, sing psalms unto him, talk ye of all his wondrous works. [10]Glory ye in his holy name: let the heart of them rejoice that seek the LORD. [11]Seek the LORD and his strength, seek his face continually. [12]Remember his marvellous works that he hath done, his wonders, and the judgments of his mouth.**

Verse 8 identifies three aspects of true worship: thanksgiving, petition, and proclamation. When we begin to worship, praise and thanksgiving are expressed. Later we **call upon his name** in petition. Finally, we **make known his deeds among the people.** Most translations have the plural "peoples" (NASB, NRSV) or something that emphasizes the broad scope of the proclamation. The proclamation is to be made within the congregation and beyond it: "Make known among the nations what he has done" (NIV). These are still the basic components of true worship of the holy God. We come together on the Lord's Day to worship, and we go forth to testify and serve.

The word **sing** occurs twice in verse 9. The faith of the Bible is a singing faith. The singing is to be directed **unto him** (the Lord Himself). David was a musician; therefore, music and singing were especially dear to him. The existence of the Book of Psalms testifies to the importance of music and singing in worship. The early Christians sang. Paul wrote, "Speak to one another with psalms, hymns and spiritual songs. Sing and make music in your heart to the Lord" (Eph. 5:19, NIV). All the great revivals of the Christian faith have been accompanied with singing. Music in worship plays a vital part, for music is a way of expressing emotions and feelings that prosaic language cannot express.

Notice that believers are called to **sing unto him, sing psalms unto him.** We are not to see acts of worship as performances for other people but as sacrifices of praise to the Lord Himself.

Glory ye in his holy name is the heart of worship—glorifying the Lord. His **name** represents God Himself. True worship exalts and honors the Lord for who He is and for what He has done. During this study, we are focusing on one of the so-called attributes of God—His holiness. We need to remember that it is not enough to say, "God is holy." We must address our prayers and songs to the **holy** God. It is one thing to say, "God is holy." However, the true language of faith is singing, "Holy, Holy, Holy" or praying, "holy Father."

The word **seek** is found three times in verses 10-11. Three aspects of worship are mentioned. First, we read, **let the heart of them rejoice that seek the LORD.** Seeking the Lord is motivated by joy and produces rejoicing. Worship ought to be joyful. Second, those who seek the Lord find the Lord's **strength.** Worship enables worshipers to find strength to live according to God's will. Third, worshipers are to **seek his face continually.** God's **face** is His presence. This is another key aspect of true worship. It involves seeking the presence of the Lord. Too often we go through the motions of private prayer and public worship without having personal communion with the Lord. A question to ask yourself as you end your prayer time or finish public worship is, "Did I seek the presence of the Lord?" If you sought His face, you surely found Him. Notice that this is to be done not once for all but **continually.** This truth is parallel to the many emphases on perseverance in prayer (Luke 11:5-13) and on the need to be faithful in worshiping with other believers (Heb. 10:25). Too many professed believers come to church only occasionally and do not make prayer a daily habit.

Remember is a key word in the Bible. Worship involves remembering what God has done for His people in biblical times and in our own lives. We do the former by opening His Word and reading of **his marvellous works that he hath done, his wonders, and the judgments of his mouth.** Thus the Bible must be a part of true worship.

To summarize, what are some lasting lessons about worship in these verses?

1. Gifted people are called to exercise their gifts in public worship.
2. Worship includes praise, petition, and proclamation.
3. Music and singing are crucial components of public worship.
4. Worship involves seeking the Lord's presence with joy and finding new strength.
5. Worship involves remembering what God has done and said.

Eternally Faithful (1 Chron. 16:15-17)

In what sense does God remember and in what sense are we to remember? What relevance do past covenants have for today? What are lasting lessons about worship?

Verses 15-17: Be ye mindful always of his covenant; the word which he commanded to a thousand generations; ¹⁶even of the covenant which he made with Abraham, and of his oath unto Isaac; ¹⁷and hath confirmed the same to Jacob for a law, and to Israel for an everlasting covenant.

Translators differ over who does the remembering. The *King James Version* follows the Hebrew text of verse 15: **Be ye mindful always of his covenant** (similarly, NASB, NRSV). Some other translations use the parallel in Psalm 105:8, in which it is God who remembers: "He remembers his covenant forever" (NIV). Both are true. God remembers His promises. This doesn't mean that He forgets them for a while and needs to recall them. It means that He keeps them constantly in mind and fulfills them in His own time and way. Humans do sometimes forget and need to remember His promises. Further,

Martin J. Selman made an important point: "Remembering in the Old Testament includes acting upon that which is recalled, and is much more than a purely intellectual exercise."[2]

David lived hundreds of years after the patriarchs. Why then did he go back to God's promises to them? These promises represented **an everlasting covenant.** Thus people of faith remember in worship and in study **the covenant which he made with Abraham.** We remember **his oath unto Isaac.** And we remember how God **confirmed the same to Jacob.** Genesis 12–50 continues to have relevance and meaning for believers in every generation.

Recalling biblical promises is part of true worship. This is one of the lasting marks of true worship.

Exclusively God (1 Chron. 16:25-29)

*How great is the Lord? Did David believe that God was the best of many gods or that He was the one God? Why is idolatry foolish? How does verse 27 use many words in an attempt to describe God? How can we **give unto the Lord the glory due unto his name**? What does it mean to **worship the Lord in the beauty of holiness**?*

Verses 25-26: **For great is the Lord, and greatly to be praised: he also is to be feared above all gods. [26]For all the gods of the people are idols: but the Lord made the heavens.**

The Bible uses the word **great** to describe **the Lord.** This word is one of many Hebrew words translated **great** in describing the Lord. He is greater than what we usually mean by the word *great*. He is the infinite, eternal God, whose ways are beyond our comprehension. Because of this, He is **greatly to be praised.** Our worship cannot begin to fathom Him or to do Him full justice. But we should try to exalt Him as best we can.

> Great is the Lord, He is holy and just;
> By His power we trust in His love.
> Great is the Lord, He is faithful and true;
> By His mercy He proves He is love.
> Great is the Lord and worthy of glory!
> Great is the Lord and worthy of praise.
> Great is the Lord; now lift up your voice,
> Now lift up your voice: Great is the Lord!
> Great is the Lord![3]

Some people say that **he also is to be feared above all gods** means that the writer of the psalm believed that God is the chief among many gods. Verse 26 shows that the writer did not believe in other gods; he was aware that others did believe in them. As for him, these other **gods** were only **idols,** a word that means "nonentities." These gods were not real. They were made by humans whereas **the LORD made the heavens.** Worship within itself can be given to false gods, which are not gods at all. True worship must be given only to the true God. Whatever people worship is their god. Only God is real. Only He is to be worshiped.

Verses 27-29: **Glory and honor are in his presence; strength and gladness are in his place. [28]Give unto the LORD, ye kindreds of the people, give unto the LORD glory and strength. [29]Give unto the LORD the glory due unto his name: bring an offering, and come before him: worship the LORD in the beauty of holiness.**

Verse 27 pulls out all the stops in using four words to describe the infinite God: **glory . . . honor . . . strength . . . gladness.** Each of these words is rich in meaning. By piling them up in one verse, the inspired writer was saying that the Lord is wonderful beyond what our words can describe. We cannot comprehend the full glory of the Lord, but we can know Him and worship Him.

We are called to **give unto the LORD glory and strength.** The unattainable goal is to **give unto the LORD the glory due unto his name. Glory** refers to the full majesty and greatness of the Lord. Our worship can never fully give Him all He deserves, but this remains the goal of worship. This objective surely rules out anything that detracts from the glory due to the Lord.

Two components of worship are in the middle of verse 29. First, worshipers are to **bring an offering.** An inner impulse of all who know the Lord is to give back to Him what He has given to us with such bounty. Second, worshipers are to **come before him.** This is where the miracle of grace comes into play. We are sinners who cannot enter into the presence of the holy God, but in His love He invites us to come. The death of Jesus Christ His Son opened access for us to come boldly to God's throne of grace, in spite of our unworthiness (Heb. 4:16).

Look back over the Focal Passage for this lesson and notice how often the word **unto** is used: "Give thanks unto the LORD" (v. 8); "Sing unto him; sing psalms unto him" (v. 9); Give unto the LORD" (three times in vv. 28-29). Here in verse 29 the words are **before him.** All of these indicate that true worship is directed **unto** the Lord and done **before** the Lord. He is the audience. Too often we think of the congregation as the audience and the worship leaders as the performers before this audience. The Bible makes clear that worship leaders are not performers and congregations are not intended to be audiences. God is the audience. The congregation and the worship leaders are the ones who direct worship to the Lord. When we think of worship leaders as performers, the congregation often are only passive observers of the performances. The people either applaud or criticize the performers. Instead, we ought to see the Lord as the One unto whom we present our singing, giving, proclaiming, and obeying.

Worship the Lord in the beauty of holiness are intriguing and challenging words. They are not easy to translate. The word for **beauty** means "adornment." The difference of opinion is whether the adornment is ours as the worshipers or the adornment is the Lord's, whom we worship. On the one hand, translations include worshiping the Lord "in holy array" (NASB), "in holy attire" (REB), or "in holy vestments" (NEBmg) or, on the other hand, "in holy splendor" (NRSV), "in the splendor of holiness" (NEB), and "in the splendor of his holiness" (NIV).

One commentator on Psalm 96:9, which has the same phrase as 1 Chronicles 16:29, adopted the former view and explains "holy array" by saying: "in such outward garb and demeanor as befits those that recognize the nature of the God they adore."[4] It is true that worshipers should come reverently before the Lord, but does this mean a poorly dressed person can't worship? James 2:1-8 seems to deny that this is true. Another way to understand the adornment as applying to the worshipers is that we must come before the Lord with a holy life (see Ps. 15). However, many other translators would prefer to see the adornment as the Lord's own splendor of holiness. The heart of worship is the Lord's own splendor.

What are the lasting lessons about worship in these verses?

1. God is greater than our ability to comprehend Him, yet we can worship Him.

2. Our worship ought to seek to give Him the glory due His name.

3. Worship includes bringing a worthy offering.

4. Worship means coming before God, unworthy though we be.

5. Worship recognizes the splendor of the holy God.

Only Savior (1 Chron. 16:34-35)

What part does God's goodness and mercy play in worship? From what does the Lord save us? How are we to respond to His salvation?

Verses 34-35: **O give thanks unto the LORD; for he is good; for his mercy endureth forever. [35]And say ye, Save us, O God of our salvation, and gather us together, and deliver us from the heathen, that we may give thanks to thy holy name, and glory in thy praise.**

Verse 34 expresses a theme of many of the psalms and the heart of our faith in God. First, it calls for us to **give thanks unto the LORD.** Expressing praise is addressing our praises to the Lord for who and what He is. Expressing thanks is expressing gratitude to Him for His many blessings to us.

The word **good** is like the word *great* when it is used of God. We use the word *good* too casually today. Just as God is greater than what our word *great* means, so is He better than what our word *good* generally implies. His goodness is another way to refer to His mercy, love, grace, and lovingkindness. **Mercy** is the Hebrew word *hesed*, used in the Old Testament to describe the kindness, mercy, love, and faithfulness of God.

Verse 34 appears at the beginning of Psalm 106. Verse 35 comes near the end of the same psalm in verse 47. In between are descriptions of the history of sinful Israel and the punishment their sins brought on them. Psalm 106:47, therefore, was a prayer for the Lord to save them or deliver them from the plight caused by their sins. Throughout Israel's history were many times when the words **Save us, O God of our salvation** would fit. They fit especially after the defeat of Judah and the exile of the survivors. Thompson wrote, "Here is a prayer that could have been particularly appropriate to the Chronicler's own day though not at all inappropriate for David's day."[5]

Looked at from the perspective of the New Testament, God in Christ is our Savior from sin and death. The deliverances of the Old Testament pointed ahead to this ultimate deliverance. When we as Christians worship, we acknowledge and worship the One who alone has saved us, is saving us, and will save us.

Ideally, we are to come to the Lord clothed in garments of holiness; however, until we experience the grace and power of the holy God, we can only come to Him as unworthy sinners who need His saving and forgiving grace. This was the experience of young Isaiah when he saw the vision of the holy God in the temple. The vision of the holy God convicted Isaiah that he was a man of unclean lips. However, even as he confessed, he was invited to allow the forgiving love of the holy God to enable him to enter the presence of the Lord (Isa. 6). Of course, after we experience God's salvation, we are empowered to live a holy life, and we continue to be able to draw near to God because of His salvation in Jesus Christ.

What are the lasting lessons about worship in these verses?
1. Thanksgiving is part of true worship.
2. We are most grateful for the Lord's love and for His saving grace.
3. Through the love of God we have access to the God who saves us.

❖ Spiritual Transformations

After the ark of the covenant was brought to Jerusalem, David appointed Asaph to lead the music. The psalm expresses worship of the holy God. He is worshiped as incomparably great, eternally faithful, exclusively God, and our only Savior.

The *Life Impact* is to help you worship the holy God. Review the lasting lessons mentioned in connection with each point in the lesson outline. Evaluate your own worship in light of the list.

*Which aspects of worship do you need to improve in your own worship?*_____

*What steps will you take to make worship of the holy God real in your life?*_____

Prayer of Commitment: Holy Father, help me to worship You in a way that is pleasing in Your sight. Amen.

[1]J. A. Thompson, "1, 2 Chronicles," in *The New American Commentary*, vol. 9 [Nashville: Broadman & Holman Publishers, 1994], 140.
[2]Martin J. Selman, *1 Chronicles*, in the Tyndale Old Testament Commentaries [Downers Grove: InterVarsity Press, 1994], 169.
[3]Michael W. Smith and Deborah D. Smith, "Great Is the Lord," *The Baptist Hymnal* [Nashville: Convention Press, 1991], No. 12.
[4]H. C. Leupold, *Exposition of the Psalms* [Grand Rapids: Baker Book House, 1969], 685.
[5]Thompson, "1, 2 Chronicles," NAC, 142.

GOD IS JUST

Background Passage: Ezekiel 2–3; 18
Focal Passage: Ezekiel 18:1-3,19-20,23-32
Key Verse: Ezekiel 18:30

❖ *Significance of the Lesson*

• The *Theme* of this lesson is that God is just; He rewards each person according to his or her ways.

• The *Life Question* addressed in this lesson is, What impact does the reality that God is just have on me?

• The *Biblical Truth* is that because God is just, every individual faces God's judgment and is accountable directly to Him.

• The *Life Impact* is to help you live in light of the reality of God's just judgment.

Is God Just?

In the secular worldview, the concept of judgment by a sovereign God in this life and after death, if perceived at all, is not taken seriously. This, however, does not keep people from blaming God for the bad things that happen to them. They believe that if God exists at all, He is unjust and uncaring.

In the biblical worldview, God is both just and merciful. God's judgment is real in this life and in the life to come. Those who are saved are saved by the grace of God. They have repented and placed their faith in Him. The eternal destiny of those who are saved is secure, but they will receive retribution for the good and bad they have done.

Ezekiel

Ezekiel was a prophet to the Jewish exiles in Babylon. He had been taken to Babylon with a group that included King Jehoiachin [jih-HOY-uh-kin] in 597 B.C. Ezekiel's messages focused on the coming judgment of God on Jerusalem in the years before the destruction of the city in 587 B.C. He had to contend with false prophets who promised that God would rescue Jerusalem from destruction and set the exiles free. After the fall of Jerusalem, his messages became more hopeful. While Ezekiel was preaching to the exiles in Babylon, Jeremiah was doing the same thing back in Judah.

Word Study: *equal, unequal*

The Hebrew word used in Ezekiel 18:25,29 to refer to whether the Lord measures human lives equally or unequally is translated into English in a variety of ways: "not just . . . unjust" (NIV), "unfair" (NRSV), "not fair" (NKJV), "not right" (NASB), "without principle" (NEB, REB). This Hebrew verb means "to measure, determine, examine." The noun means "measure" or "amount." This is not the usual word that the Old Testament uses for God as just or unjust *(mishpat).*

❖ *Search the Scriptures*

God told the people to quit using the proverb, **"The fathers have eaten sour grapes, and the children's teeth are set on edge."** God said that each person is accountable for individual sins. The good son of a bad father will not be judged for his father's sins, and the good father of a bad son will not be judged for his son's sins. When the people accused God of being unjust, He charged that it was they who were unjust. He will not spare the good person who turns to a life of continuous sin. The bad person who repents and turns from sin to righteousness will live. God pleaded with sinners to repent so they would live.

An Irresponsible Attitude (Ezek. 18:1-3)

*How were the people using the **proverb** in verse 2? Why did God tell them to cease using it?*

Verses 1-3: The word of the LORD came unto me again, saying, ²What mean ye, that ye use this proverb concerning the land of Israel, saying, The fathers have eaten sour grapes, and the children's teeth are set on edge? ³As I live, saith the Lord GOD, ye shall not have occasion anymore to use this proverb in Israel.

Verse 1 introduces **the word of the LORD** that was delivered in the rest of this chapter. The **proverb** was a familiar couplet or saying in that day. This is clear since the same saying is mentioned in Jeremiah 31:29. Jeremiah referred to a future time when the people would no longer use this proverb. Ezekiel quoted the Lord as telling the exiles to quit using it right away. What was God's objection to the way the people used the proverb?

The rest of Ezekiel 18 seems to show that the people were reciting this saying to explain why they were being punished with exile from their homeland. They were saying, in effect, that their forefathers had sinned and they were being punished because of their forefathers' sins.

The people must have felt they were justified in this conclusion by the earlier history of Israel. For example, in two of God's key teachings to their forefathers He had spoken of the sins of one generation being visited on succeeding generations. The Second Commandment is followed by the warning to those who make graven images: "I the LORD thy God am a jealous God, visiting the iniquity of the fathers upon the children unto the third and fourth generation of them that hate me" (Ex. 20:5). In one of the highpoints of Old Testament revelation, God revealed to Moses the name of the Lord. After emphasizing the love and forgiveness of God, the Lord added, "and that will by no means clear the guilty; visiting the iniquity of the fathers upon the children, and upon the children's children, unto the third and to the fourth generation" (Ex. 34:7).

The people also could have quoted Ezekiel and other prophets who had proclaimed that the Israelites' sins had led to the exile. During the long, evil reign of King Manasseh, the prophets announced that the fate of the nation was sealed (2 Kings 21:11-15). Thus the people could cite these instances of the dire effect of their forefathers' sins. In doing so, they implied that they were innocent victims of the sins of past generations. This was a false assumption. That generation had sins of its own for which to be punished. In condemning them, God was not denying the evil influence of past generations, but He was condemning the human tendency to refuse to admit our own guilt and to blame our troubles on someone or something else. Some people blame their parents for how they turned out. Others blame society as a whole. Some blame friends. Some blame God. Some blame the devil. Many people say such things as: "It's not my fault." "I'm not to blame." "I couldn't help it." They find it hard to say: "I have sinned." "It is my fault." "I am to blame." "I could have helped it." God told the people to quit blaming their plight on others.

What lasting lessons are in these verses?

1. Rather than confessing their own sins, people try to blame others.

2. God denied that anyone could escape personal guilt by blaming others. Such is an irresponsible attitude.

An Individual Accountability (Ezek. 18:19-20)

What did the people mean by the first part of verse 19? What is the central meaning of verses 19-20?

Verses 19-20: Yet say ye, Why? doth not the son bear the iniquity of the father? When the son hath done that which is lawful and right, and hath kept all my statutes, and hath done them, he shall surely live. [20]The soul that sinneth, it shall die. The son shall not bear the iniquity of the father, neither shall the father bear the iniquity of the son: the righteousness of the righteous shall be upon him, and the wickedness of the wicked shall be upon him.

Verse 19a is the second of three sayings of the people in the chapter (vv. 2,25). The people seem to have been denying that their experience matched what Ezekiel said. They thought of themselves as good people of evil fathers, yet they were being punished for the sins of their fathers. This is different from what Ezekiel said in verses 14-18. Verse 19b is God's reaffirmation of verses 14-18. When a good **son hath done that which is lawful and right . . . he shall surely live.**

In the words **the soul that sinneth, it shall die,** the Hebrew word *nephesh* refers to the total person, not just to the spirit or ethereal portion of a person. "The word 'soul' here carries the meaning 'life' or 'person' and should not be confused with the concept of a 'soul' as the spiritual and eternal part of a person."[1] Thus it can be translated, "The person who sins will die" (NASB). The issue at stake here is not necessarily eternal salvation.

The **iniquity** of neither **the son** nor **the father** will be borne by the other. Verse 20b puts it another way, "The righteousness of the righteous man will be credited to him, and the wickedness of the wicked will be charged against him" (NIV). This is another way of stating the personal accountability of each person. None of us can blame either our sons or our fathers and thus excuse our own sins. Neither can any of us assume that the good life of our sons or our fathers will be able to make us righteous.

This teaching of individual accountability does not mean that we are not influenced by the good or the evil of others—especially of our families. Without question we are influenced, yet this does not change the fact that we make our own choices.

Our society tends to excuse personal accountability based on a secular doctrine of determinism in which naturalistic forces over which one has no control sweep the person helplessly along. People are considered victims of physical, social, and economic forces that shape their lives and destiny. In his novel *An American Tragedy*, Theodore Dreiser told the story of Clyde Griffiths, a hapless victim of such forces. Dreiser tells of the many forces that shaped Clyde. He got a girl pregnant, met a more wealthy and attractive girl, and murdered the pregnant girl. As Dreiser told the story of this man's life, he presented him as a prisoner of his environment. At the man's trial, one of his lawyers said to Clyde, "You didn't make yourself, did you, Clyde?"[2] How often do we hear this type of excuse raised as a defense in criminal trials?

What are the lasting lessons in these verses?

1. People often want to blame their suffering on the actions of others rather than on their own actions and sins.

2. God said that each person is accountable for his or her own sins.

A Just God (Ezek. 18:23-29)

What kind of God is revealed in verse 23? Why did the people accuse God of being unjust? Why did God accuse the people of being unjust?

Verses 23-24: Have I any pleasure at all that the wicked should die? saith the Lord GOD: and not that he should return from his ways, and live? 24But when the righteous turneth away from his righteousness, and committeth iniquity, and doeth according to all the abominations that the wicked man doeth, shall he live? All his righteousness that he hath done shall not be mentioned: in his trespass that he hath trespassed, and in his sin that he hath sinned, in them shall he die.

A new element enters the chapter in verses 21-24. The possibility of repentance and change of life from sin to righteousness is mentioned in verses 21-22. Verse 23 reveals the mercy of God. He takes no **pleasure at all that the wicked should die.** Instead, His joy is in seeing a sinner **return from his ways, and live.** This love of God for sinners and the possibility of conversion are elaborated on in verses 30-32.

Verse 24 is a warning against presumption, a warning that is found in both Testaments. The verse takes the opposite situation from the one in verses 21-22. The picture there was of a wicked person repenting and becoming a righteous person. In verse 24 **the righteous** person turns to evil and becomes a **wicked** person. Notice how serious are the person's sins. He commits **all the abominations that the wicked man doeth.** The Lord asked, **Shall he live?** The clear answer is no—**In his sin that he hath sinned, in them shall he die.**

The doctrines of election and security are not doctrines of presumption that condone a life of sin. Those who turn from what appears to be a righteous life to an ungodly life and continue in it are either badly backslidden or they have never experienced God's saving grace. Jesus warned that just professing His name did not ensure salvation (Matt. 7:21). And Paul wrote, "Examine yourselves, whether ye be in the faith; prove your own selves. Know ye not your own selves, how that Jesus Christ is in you, except ye be reprobates?" (2 Cor. 13:5).

Verses 25-29: Yet ye say, The way of the Lord is not equal. Hear now, O house of Israel; Is not my way equal? are not your ways unequal? [26]When a righteous man turneth away from his righteousness, and committeth iniquity, and dieth in them; for his iniquity that he hath done shall he die. [27]Again, when the wicked man turneth away from his wickedness that he hath committed, and doeth that which is lawful and right, he shall save his soul alive. [28]Because he considereth, and turneth away from all his transgressions that he hath committed, he shall surely live, he shall not die. [29]Yet saith the house of Israel, The way of the Lord is not equal. O house of Israel, are not my ways equal? are not your ways unequal?

The third saying of the people is quoted in verse 25. They were saying, **The way of the Lord is not equal** ("just," NIV, "right" NASB, "fair" NKJV). They were still claiming that God had punished them for the sins of their evil forefathers. In doing this, God was not being just or fair. They also seem to have added to their list that forgiving sinners was not just. This forgiveness allows a formerly evil person to be spared while more righteous people, who seemed to need no repentance, are punished.

To this accusation, God made a countercharge. He was not unjust; they were. They had been claiming to be righteous people who were being punished for the sins of their evil forefathers. But the truth of the matter was that they were at least as guilty as, if not more guilty than, their ancestors. They were in exile because of their own sins.

God reaffirmed the truths of verses 21-24 in verses 26-28. Verse 26 reinforces verses 24. **When a righteous man** turns from **righteousness** to live a wicked life, he is punished for the sins he has committed. His past goodness does not compensate for his persistent sinning. Verses 27-28 reinforce verses 21-22. **When the wicked man turneth away from his wickedness,** is God unjust for forgiving him and allowing him to show his changed life by his righteous actions?

God is just in condemning persistent sinners who reject His love, and He is just in forgiving repentant sinners based on His mercy—which is fully revealed in the cross. Some people demand to receive only what they deserve. They are making a big mistake.

C. S. Lewis wrote the imaginative story of a group of hell-bound spirits who end up temporarily in heaven. The title of the book, *The Great Divorce,* refers to the vast gulf fixed between heaven and hell. Lewis' story makes this point in a striking way. He showed that the hell-bound spirits do not fit in heaven. They spend their time complaining and seeking to justify themselves. Lewis described one hell-bound spirit who encountered the spirit of a murderer on earth—but one who had repented and was changed by God's grace. The hell-bound spirit was outraged at the injustice of him—a good man—on the way to hell while the sinner was in heaven. Seeking to justify himself, he said, "I'm a decent man and if I had my rights I'd have been here long ago and you can tell them I said so."

The saved sinner replied, "It isn't exactly true, you know."

The other asked, "What isn't true?"

"You weren't a decent man and you didn't do your best. We none of us were and we none of us did."[3]

The same is true of each of us in the moral and spiritual realm. We need mercy, not justice. If God gave us what we deserved, all of us would be in trouble.

What lasting lessons are in these verses?

1. Wicked people who repent and then live a righteous life will live.

2. Righteous people who turn into and persist in a wicked life will be punished for their sins.

3. People accuse God of being unjust.

4. God accuses sinful people of being unjust.

5. The justice and mercy of God go together.

A Call to Repent (Ezek. 18:30-32)

*What does it mean that God is Judge of all people? What is repentance? How does true repentance lead to **a new heart and a new spirit**? How do these verses reveal the attitude of God toward sinners?*

Verses 30-32: **Therefore I will judge you, O house of Israel, every-one according to his ways, saith the Lord GOD. Repent, and turn your-selves from all your transgressions; so iniquity shall not be your ruin. ³¹Cast away from you all your transgressions, whereby ye have trans-gressed; and make you a new heart and a new spirit: for why will ye die, O house of Israel? ³²For I have no pleasure in the death of him that dieth, saith the Lord GOD: wherefore turn yourselves, and live ye.**

The first part of verse 30 makes explicit what is implicit throughout the chapter. God **will judge . . . everyone according to his ways.** No one will escape God's judgment. The New Testament makes clear that the judgment of true believers will not end in eternal condemnation, but the judgment of those who reject Christ will result in eternal condemnation. The Bible also makes clear that the saved will be judged according to their stewardship of life (see Rom. 14:10-12; 1 Cor. 3:11-15; 2 Cor. 5:10).

But God yearns to save, not condemn, sinners. **Repent, and turn** translate the same Hebrew word into different English words. The word *shub* means "to turn." The *New English Bible* preserves this repetition, "Turn, turn from your offences." They were told: **Cast away from you all your transgressions.** The ultimate purpose of this chap-ter is not to condemn sinners but to call them to repentance so God can forgive them and create in them **a new heart and a new spirit.** Actually, in verse 31 Ezekiel called on them to **make you a new heart and a new spirit.** Ezekiel referred to this new heart elsewhere and made it dependent on the grace and power of God (11:19; 36:26-27). The people could make it possible by repenting and by allowing God to make them a new life, beginning from within.

The options were to repent and live or to refuse to repent and die. God is pictured as Judge in verse 30, but He is pictured as a loving Father in verse 32. God's loving heart is revealed in this verse. He takes **no pleasure in the death of** the wicked. As verse 23 indicated, His joy is in the repentance of sinners. Ezekiel 33 is parallel to chapter 18 in many ways. Ezekiel 33:11 brings it all together: "As I live, saith the Lord GOD, I have no pleasure in the death of the wicked; but that the wicked turn from his way and live: turn ye, turn ye from your evil ways; for why will ye die, O house of Israel?"

Many people fail to heed the warning because they believe they are already righteous. Only people who confess their sins and trust in the Lord will be forgiven.

What lasting lessons are in these verses?

1. God is Judge of all people.
2. He pleads with people to repent.
3. Without repentance, people will perish.
4. God is a loving Father who pleads for sinners to repent and live, not to reject Him and die.

❖ *Spiritual Transformations*

Ezekiel delivered the word of the Lord that warned against further use of the proverb, "The fathers have eaten sour grapes, and the children's teeth are set on edge." God taught that each person is accountable for his or her own sins. Included in this is the idea that no person can rely on his father's or his son's goodness—or even on his own past goodness. When the people accused God of being unjust in His judgments, the Lord accused them of being unjust. God is Judge of all people, but He yearns to see people repent and live rather than refuse to repent and perish.

What can you do to live in light of God's just judgment? Each of the four parts of the outline has an answer: (1) Don't seek to blame anyone but yourself for your sins; (2) Accept personal accountability for your actions; (3) Realize that God is just and merciful; and (4) Heed the Lord's call and repent of your sins.

Which of these points, or which of the lasting truths, speaks to you most? _____

What actions does this fact call for on your behalf? _____
_____

How can I believe in a just God after the events of September 11, 2001? How does this lesson help me affirm the biblical teaching that God is just? _____

Prayer of Commitment: Merciful and just God, forgive my sins and create in me a new heart and a new spirit. Amen.

---

[1]Lamar Eugene Cooper, Sr., "Ezekiel," in *The New American Commentary*, vol. 17 [Nashville: Broadman & Holman Publishers, 1994], 188-189.

[2]Quoted by Randall Stewart, *American Literature and Christian Doctrine* [Baton Rouge: Louisiana State University, 1958], 119.

[3]C. S. Lewis, *The Great Divorce* [New York: The Macmillan Company, 1946], 34-35.

GOD IS PATIENT

Background Passage: Jonah 1:1–4:11; 2 Peter 3:1-18
Focal Passage: Jonah 3:1-3a,10; 4:1-3,6-11; 2 Peter 3:9,15
Key Verse: 2 Peter 3:9

❖ *Significance of the Lesson*

• The *Theme* of this lesson is that God is patient; He does not want anyone to perish but for all to repent.

• The *Life Question* this lesson seeks to address is, Why doesn't a just God immediately put an end to evil?

• The *Biblical Truth* is that God patiently delays judgment because He desires that all people repent.

• The *Life Impact* is to help you faithfully share the gospel as God patiently delays judgment.

How Patient Is God?

In the secular worldview, if God is viewed as existing at all, He is perceived as remote, uninvolved, and even lacking the power to effect judgment. Some secular people view God as indulgent of human sin.

In the biblical worldview, the all-powerful and just God patiently delays judgment because He desires all people to repent. His patience is not passive waiting but active movement designed to call people to repent. In showing such patience, He forebears with the sins of people.

Word Study: *longsuffering*

The word translated **longsuffering** in 2 Peter 3:9 is the Greek verb *makrothumeo.* The same English word in verse 15 is a translation of the related Greek noun *makrothumia.* These words come from *makros,* meaning "far away in distance or in time," and *thumoo,* meaning "to make angry." Thus although the words in 2 Peter are often translated "patient" and "patience" (NIV), the Greek words do not refer to patience in the sense of passive waiting but to forbearance in the sense of putting up with evil people for a long time. The comparable word in the Old Testament is a combination of two Hebrew words: 'erek, meaning "long," and 'appayim, meaning "nose." The idiom for anger in the Old Testament is literally "the nose burns." The idiom for "long-suffering" or being "slow to anger" is "long of nose." The words 'erek 'appayim are found in Exodus 34:6, which is quoted in Jonah 4:2.

❖ Search the Scriptures

When God called Jonah the second time, he obeyed the call to go to Nineveh and preach. After Jonah preached judgment, the people of Nineveh repented and God relented from His warning of destruction. Jonah was angry with God. When he prayed, he explained why he had been reluctant to go to Nineveh and why the Ninevites' repentance and God's forgiveness made him angry. Jonah knew that God was a longsuffering and merciful God, and he feared God would spare the people of Nineveh, whom the prophet hated. When Jonah waited in the hot sun, hoping for God to destroy the city, God caused a vine to grow and provide shade for Jonah. Then God sent a worm to destroy the vine. When Jonah was angry about the loss of the vine, God asked if He was not justified in showing as much concern for the multitudes in Nineveh as Jonah had shown for the vine.

When some false teachers mocked the promise of the Lord's coming by pointing to what seemed an unreasonable delay, God through Peter responded by explaining that God's seeming delay was actually an example of His forbearance based on His desire that all come to repentance.

Patient God (Jonah 3:1-3a,10)

*How did God show His forbearing patience toward Jonah? Why did Jonah go to Nineveh **the second time** God told him to go? In what sense did God **repent**? How did God show His forbearing patience toward Nineveh?*

Jonah 3:1-3a: And the word of the LORD came unto Jonah the second time, saying, ²Arise, go unto Nineveh, that great city, and preach unto it the preaching that I bid thee. ³ªSo Jonah arose, and went unto Nineveh, according to the word of the LORD.

Jonah 3:1-2 indicates this was **the second time** that **the word of the LORD came unto Jonah** and told him to **go unto to Nineveh.** The first time was in 1:1-2. When the initial call came, the prophet turned and went the opposite direction from Nineveh. The rebellious prophet had been through a storm, been thrown overboard, been swallowed by a big fish, and finally vomited back on the coast from which he had sailed. Now he heard the Lord call him to go the Nineveh **the second time.**

This second call is almost the same as 1:1-2. Jonah 3:1 is the same except that 1:1 contains the name of Jonah's father and 3:1 says **the second time.** Jonah 3:2 is similar to 1:2 except for two things. First, a different preposition is used. Jonah 1:2 says to "cry against it" and 3:2 says to **preach unto it.** The main difference, however, is the addition to 1:2 of the words "for their wickedness is come up before me." The biggest difference comes between 1:3 and 3:3. In 1:3 when Jonah was called, he "rose up to flee unto Tarshish from the presence of the Lord." In 3:3 **Jonah arose, and went unto Nineveh, according to the word of the Lord.**

The point of these verses in this lesson is the patient longsuffering of the Lord in dealing with His prophet Jonah. This patient longsuffering had not involved mere passive waiting for Jonah to change his mind on his own. The Lord had used His sovereign power to send a storm and a great fish to rescue Jonah from drowning and to vomit the reluctant prophet back on the coast from which he had set sail in running from the Lord.

The lesson for those whom the Lord calls is to heed His call. If you are running from God's call and He gives you a second chance, take it. God is the God of more than one opportunity to follow Him. This is a mark of His forbearance. God put up with Jonah's rebellion and disobedience, but God did not give up on the prophet.

Jonah 3:10: **And God saw their works, that they turned from their evil way; and God repented of the evil, that he had said that he would do unto them; and he did it not.**

Jonah went through Nineveh warning that destruction was coming in 40 days. Amazingly this evil city responded to the warning from the reluctant prophet. This miracle is even greater than Jonah's being kept alive in the fish. Nineveh was among the most evil cities of all times. Yet everyone—high and low—**turned from their evil way. Turned** is *shub,* the usual Old Testament word for "repent." The *King James Version* uses the English word **repented** to describe God's action. This is a different Hebrew word that means "relented" (NASB, NKJV). "Whereas the English term 'repent' conveys the idea of a change of behaviour from worse to better, the Hebrew verb *niham* refers rather to a decision to act otherwise, and does not necessarily imply that the first action is inferior to the second. The English verb 'relent' conveys better the meaning of the Hebrew."[1]

This verse illustrates the longsuffering love of God for the worst of people. God went to considerable trouble to send Jonah to the people of Nineveh. He had to endure much evil from them. Yet He acted in patient love to give the people of Nineveh an opportunity to repent.

What are the lasting truths in these verses?

1. God shows patient forbearance toward His own people and toward the lost sinners of the world.

2. God often gives His people more than one opportunity to obey His call.

3. God deals with us not with passive waiting but with active measures designed to lead us to do His will.

4. Believers should obey when the Lord calls.

5. Believers should take the Lord's Word to evil people who have not heard His message to repent.

6. God sometimes relents of His warnings of destruction when people turn from their sins.

Angry Prophet (Jonah 4:1-3)

Why was Jonah so angry? Why did God listen to a prayer from such an angry servant of His? What Old Testament passage did Jonah quote? What does verse 2 reveal about God's patience? Why did Jonah run from God's first call? Why did Jonah feel about the people of Nineveh the way he did? How could God use a messenger whose motives were so bad?

Jonah 4:1-3: But it displeased Jonah exceedingly, and he was very angry. [2]And he prayed unto the Lord, and said, I pray thee, O Lord, was not this my saying, when I was yet in my country? Therefore I fled before unto Tarshish: for I knew that thou art a gracious God, and merciful, slow to anger, and of great kindness, and repentest thee of the evil. [3]Therefore now, O Lord, take, I beseech thee, my life from me; for it is better for me to die than to live.

Notice how verse 1 piles up words to show Jonah's deep emotion: **It displeased Jonah exceedingly, and he was very angry.** This was a strange reaction for a missionary who had seen all the people of a vast city repent. We might expect the book to end happily with 3:10. It must be a surprise to first-time readers of the Book of Jonah when they come to chapter 4. Most missionaries rejoice when even a few lost people repent. The reason for Jonah's anger is never fully explained, but the depth of it becomes clear as chapter 4 unfolds. The reason for his anger lies in the history of the times. Nineveh was the capital of the Assyrian Empire, probably the most ruthless conquerors of ancient history. They eventually overwhelmed Israel, which was Jonah's country.

Verse 2 is a quotation of the first part of one of the most famous passages in the Old Testament—Exodus 34:6-7. The Lord spoke these words to Moses when Moses asked the Lord His name. Israel had sinned by making the golden calf, and Moses was seeking assurance that the Lord would not destroy His rebellious people. This passage is quoted in all three divisions of the Hebrew Old Testament (Num. 14:18; Neh. 9:17; Pss. 86:15; 103:8; 145:8; Joel 2:13; Jonah 4:2; and Nahum 1:3). After quoting the first part of the famous saying, Jonah added **and repentest thee of the evil. Repentest** means "relents" (NIV, NKJV).

The key words for this lesson on God's patience are **slow to anger.** As noted in the "Word Study," **slow to anger** is the Old Testament equivalent of "longsuffering" in the New Testament. The origins and basic meanings of both the Hebrew and Greek words are similar. Both go beyond the idea of passive waiting to include forbearance and actions designed to give people every opportunity to repent. The words **slow to anger** come in a context that shows the close relation of this quality to the love of God—which is described by several words, including *hesed,* the Hebrew word for lovingkindness.

Such was God's attitude toward the people of Nineveh. He showed Himself to be **a gracious God, and merciful, slow to anger, and of great kindness.** Although Jonah spoke these words as **he prayed unto the LORD,** his was an angry prayer. Others rejoiced when they quoted Exodus 34:6, but Jonah complained. These words were not praise to the Lord but a tirade against Him.

For the first time in the book, Jonah explained why he had fled from God's first call to go to Nineveh. He fled because he knew God was loving and forbearing toward sinners; and he feared that if they heard God's word, they would repent and God would forgive them. That is the kind of God He is. Now Jonah had obeyed God, and his worst fears were confirmed. By some miracle, the evil people had repented and God had removed His threat to destroy them. Jonah was so upset that he asked, **O LORD, take, I beseech thee, my life from me; for it is better for me to die than to live.**

Jonah 4:1-3 shows again the longsuffering patience of the Lord toward not only the people of Nineveh but also toward His angry, complaining prophet. The people of the Old Testament used candor and honesty in their prayers to God. Jonah's honest expression of feelings borders on blasphemy. His prayer certainly was selfish. The word "I" or "my" occurs at least nine times in the original. Yet the Lord put up with Jonah's anger and self-pity. That is pure forbearance.

Jonah's motives for preaching in Nineveh were wrong, but God still used him to accomplish His purpose. God can use those who do what He commands, even if they do it out of wrong motives. But they miss His blessing and the enjoyment that comes from it.

What are the lasting lessons in these verses?

1. God is loving and longsuffering in seeking to lead people to repentance.

2. God's servants sometimes lack His kind of forbearing love for sinners.

3. God is longsuffering with the misplaced hatred and prejudice of His people.

4. God sometimes uses servants with wrong motives, but the servants miss God's blessing.

Sovereign Lord (Jonah 4:6-9)

What did Jonah hope would happen as he waited and watched? How do these verses reveal the sovereignty of God? What made Jonah glad? Why did God destroy the vine? How does God use the circumstances of life to try to teach us His lessons? How did God continue to show His longsuffering toward Jonah and the people of Nineveh?

Jonah 4:6-9: And the LORD God prepared a gourd, and made it to come up over Jonah, that it might be a shadow over his head, to deliver him from his grief. So Jonah was exceeding glad of the gourd. [7]But God prepared a worm when the morning rose the next day, and it smote the gourd that it withered. [8]And it came to pass, when the sun did arise, that God prepared a vehement east wind; and the sun beat upon the head of Jonah, that he fainted, and wished in himself to die, and said, It is better for me to die than to live. [9]And God said to Jonah, Doest thou well to be angry for the gourd? And he said, I do well to be angry, even unto death.

God asked Jonah if he were doing right by being angry. The angry prophet built a shelter on a hill overlooking Nineveh and waited to see what would happen (vv. 4-5). He may have thought that the people of Nineveh would reveal the superficiality of their repentance and God would destroy them.

The repetition of **prepared** is significant: **the Lord God prepared a gourd . . . God prepared a worm . . . God prepared a vehement east wind. Prepared** stresses divine initiative and sovereignty. The **gourd** or "vine" (NIV) grew quickly and provided comfort for Jonah by shading him from the fierce sun—**so Jonah was exceeding glad of the gourd.** This is the only time in the book that it says Jonah was **glad**—and it was a selfish gladness over his own comfort.

But God also **prepared a worm** that destroyed the vine, leaving Jonah in the blazing sun. God further added to the prophet's misery when He **prepared a vehement** ("scorching," NIV) **east wind; and the sun beat upon the head of Jonah, that he fainted, and wished in himself to die.** For the second time (see v. 4) God asked Jonah, **Doest thou well to be angry?** or "Do you have a right to be angry?" (NIV). This time God's question related to the gourd or vine. Jonah quickly answered that he did have a right to be angry and that he was angry enough to die.

God was using His sovereign power to try to teach the angry prophet some of the lessons of life. One lesson was Jonah's dependence on the Lord. Another was the need to be grateful for little things. Still another was the greater value of people than things. Up to this point, the prophet had not learned the Lord's lessons.

Throughout verses 4-9, the Lord continued to show His amazing longsuffering toward the angry, selfish, sulking, ungrateful, and complaining prophet. Just look at all the Lord put up with even as He continued to deal mercifully with Jonah!

What are the lasting lessons of these verses?

1. God has sovereign power over all things.
2. God uses the school of life to seek to teach people the lessons of life.
3. Some of God's people are slow to learn the lessons of life.
4. God continues to show forbearance toward His people.

Merciful Savior (Jonah 4:10-11; 2 Pet. 3:9,15)

*What question did the Lord ask Jonah at the end of the book? Why does the Bible not tell us how Jonah responded? What question was 2 Peter 3:9 designed to answer? What does 2 Peter 3:9 reveal about God? How is **the longsuffering of our Lord** related to **salvation**?*

Jonah 4:10-11: **Then said the LORD, Thou hast had pity on the gourd, for the which thou hast not labored, neither madest it grow; which came up in a night, and perished in a night: ¹¹And should not I spare Nineveh, that great city, wherein are more than sixscore thousand persons that cannot discern between their right hand and their left hand; and also much cattle?**

These verses spell out the main lesson that God was seeking to teach Jonah and Israel. God contrasted Jonah's **pity on the gourd** with his lack of pity for the multitudes of people in Nineveh. The word for **pity** or "compassion" (NASB)—"concerned" (NIV)—is used in verse 10 of Jonah's feeling for the vine. Other translations bring out more clearly God's feeling toward the people of Nineveh in verse 11 in contrast to Jonah's feeling in verse 10: "You had compassion on the plant for which you did not work and which you did not cause to grow, which came up overnight and perished overnight. Should I not have compassion on Nineveh, the great city in which there are more than 120,000 persons who do not know the difference between their right and left hand, as well as many animals?" (NASB).

Notice the sharp contrast. Jonah was concerned about a vine, but God was concerned about thousands of people. Jonah's vine brought him one day of comfort; the eternal welfare of many people was at stake in Nineveh.

Bible students ponder the meaning of the words **cannot discern between their right hand and their left hand.** Some believe this refers to children. The question this raises is, "If Nineveh had 120,000 children, what was the total population?" Therefore, other Bible students think the words refer to the limited moral discernment of these pagan people. In either case, the basic question to Jonah was clear. He was concerned about a vine that brought him only one day's gladness; God was concerned about the lives and destinies of many people. Which was more important?

The curtain falls after verse 11. Readers of the Book of Jonah are not told how Jonah responded to God's appeal in verses 10-11. Jonah represented the attitude of his fellow Israelites to pagan Gentiles. Each Israelite who read the story of Jonah should have seen himself in Jonah. Thus each reader or hearer wrote his own ending to the story by his or her response. Each of us today writes his or her own ending to the Book of Jonah. If we refuse to love the people whom God loves and refuse to act to win them to Him, we write a sad and tragic ending—tragic for us and for the lost people of the world. What ending are you writing?

2 Peter 3:9,15: **The Lord is not slack concerning his promise, as some men count slackness; but is longsuffering to us-ward, not willing that any should perish, but that all should come to repentance.**

. . . .

[15]And account that the longsuffering of our Lord is salvation; even as our beloved brother Paul also according to the wisdom given unto him hath written unto you.

Peter warned of scoffers who mockingly asked about the seeming delay in the Lord's coming (vv. 3-4). Peter gave four answers. First of all, the world experienced judgment during the great flood, and it will end by fire (vv. 5-7). Second, the Lord does not measure time as we do (v. 8). Third, **the Lord is not slack concerning his promise, as some men count slackness; but is longsuffering to us-ward, not willing that any should perish, but that all should come to repentance. Slack** means "slow." The Lord is not slow to keep His promises, but He is slow to anger. **Longsuffering** means "slow to be made angry." Fourth, the day of the Lord will come in the Lord's own time. When He comes, judgment will fall on those who have rejected His longsuffering love. But for those of us who have believed, **the longsuffering of our Lord is salvation** (vv. 10-15).

Suppose the Lord had come back before you were saved. What a tragedy! Through His longsuffering, the Lord is giving people opportunity to repent and experience salvation. Peter said that Paul mentioned this in his letters too. In passages such as Romans 2:4 and 9:22 Paul used the word for **longsuffering.** In 1 Timothy 1:16 Paul used himself as an example of the Lord's longsuffering. The Lord put up with many sins by Saul of Tarsus, and He continued to seek him until he was saved.

One of the key motives for missions and evangelism is that the Lord is delaying His coming so as many as possible will hear the good news and be saved. This provides opportunities for believers to keep sharing the good news with the lost. Are you doing your part to spread this good news?

What are the lasting lessons of these verses?

1. Each of us needs to decide for him or herself which is more important—things or people?

2. God gives us the privilege of sharing His love with all people.

3. The seeming delay in the Lord's return is because of the long-suffering of the Lord. He is not willing that any perish but that all come to repentance.

4. As believers, we must send and tell the good news while we have the opportunity to do so.

❖ *Spiritual Transformations*

What does this lesson show us about the patience of God?

First, patience or forbearance is an expression of God's love. We see this in the way **slow to anger** in Jonah 4:2 is linked with **a gracious God, and merciful, slow to anger, and of great kindness.** We see it in 2 Peter 3:9, where God's **longsuffering** indicates that He is **not willing that any should perish, but that all should come to repentance.**

Second, the words in these passages do not refer to God's passive waiting but to His active involvement to lead people to do His will. When Jonah fled from God, the Lord went after him. Look at all the Lord did to bring Jonah back into His will. He did not wait for the lost world to save itself or even to seek Him, but He sent His Son to die for our sins. And He still seeks to lead each one to repentance.

Third, the Lord puts up with much that tries His patience. He put up with Jonah's anger and self-pity. He puts up with the sinners of the world.

Fourth, the longsuffering of the Lord does not mean that He is indulgent about sin. Although He is longsuffering, the time comes when judgment falls. The Book of Nahum shows how it came on Nineveh. Second Peter 3:10-16 shows how it will come on the impenitent.

Earlier we noticed that the Book of Jonah ends without telling Jonah's response and that each of us writes our own ending by how we respond to God's longsuffering love for us and for a lost world.

What ending are you writing to your own experience of God's forbearing love for you? _____

How are you sharing God's love with an unloving world? _____

_____

Prayer of Commitment: Merciful Lord, I thank You for Your longsuffering love for me and for all people. Help me experience and share Your love with all people. Amen.

---

[1]T. Desmond Alexander, "Jonah," in *Obadiah, Jonah, Micah,* in the Tyndale Old Testament Commentaries [Downers Grove: InterVarsity Press, 1988], 124.

Week of September 22

GOD FORGIVES

Background Passage: 2 Samuel 11:1–12:13; Psalm 51
Focal Passage: Psalm 51:1-17
Key Verse: Psalm 51:2

❖ *Significance of the Lesson*

• The *Theme* for this lesson is that God is forgiving; He restores those who repent.
• The *Life Question* this lesson seeks to address is, How can I experience God's forgiveness after I've sinned?
• The *Biblical Truth* is that God forgives those who humbly and honestly confess their sins and depend solely on His grace.
• The *Life Impact* is to help you accept God's forgiveness.

Views on God's Forgiveness

In a secular worldview, sin is generally viewed as an outdated concept. If failures or weaknesses are acknowledged at all, they are blamed on heredity or other forces beyond a person's control. Some people laugh at sin and those who take sin seriously. They try to justify their sins by saying such things as "everybody's doing it."

In a biblical worldview, sin is taken seriously because it separates people from God and from others. We sin when we violate or fail to measure up to the guidelines God has given us. Forgiveness is necessary for the broken relationship to be repaired.

Word Study: *blot out*

The Hebrew word *maha* means to "wipe out," "wipe away," or "blot out." Before the flood, God spoke of blotting out the lives of sinful humanity (Gen. 6:7). At times the Hebrew word was used of removing names from God's book (Ex. 32:32-33; Ps. 69:28). David used this word to describe the blotting out of his sins.

David's Sins and Confession

The superscription of Psalm 51 says that it is "a psalm of David, when Nathan the prophet came unto him, after he had gone in to Bathsheba." The biblical account of David's two great sins, Nathan's confrontation of the king, and David's confession are in 2 Samuel 11:1–12:13. David saw Bathsheba bathing on a rooftop. He sent for her and committed adultery with the wife of Uriah. When she later told David she was pregnant, David sought to lure Uriah home to spend time with his wife; but these efforts failed. Then the king sent a letter to Joab, his general, telling him to place Uriah where he would be killed. David's sin with Bathsheba may have been impulsive, but Uriah's murder was cold and calculated.

For months David tried to hide his sin. He did not confess it to God. Then Nathan came and told David of a situation of obvious injustice. When David said that the man who did what Nathan described ought to be killed, Nathan said, "Thou art the man." Then the prophet boldly pronounced God's judgment on David. The king confessed, "I have sinned." Psalm 51 represents David's confession in a prayer for forgiveness.

❖ *Search the Scriptures*

David asked the merciful God to blot out his sins. He acknowledged his sins and confessed how sinful he had been. He asked for a clean heart and a right spirit, and he promised to serve God by testifying to others. The four points in the Focal Passage Outline answer the question, "How can I experience God's forgiveness after I've sinned?"

Seek Forgiveness (Ps. 51:1-2)

In what three ways did David describe the One from whom he sought forgiveness? In what three ways did he describe that from which he needed to be forgiven? In what three ways did he describe the process of forgiveness?

Verses 1-2: Have mercy upon me, O God, according to thy loving-kindness: according unto the multitude of thy tender mercies blot out my transgressions. ²Wash me thoroughly from mine iniquity, and cleanse me from my sin.

Verses 1-2 present the themes of Psalm 51. Notice three things: (1) words that express the basis for David's hope of forgiveness, (2) words that describe his sins, and (3) words used to ask for forgiveness.

David knew that his hope for forgiveness depended on God's character, which he proceeded to describe in three expressions. The first term he used was **mercy** *(chanan)*. David knew better than to base his appeal on his own merit; therefore, he based it on the solid fact of God's mercy. David did not seek to remind God of past good things that he had done. He was too aware of the heavy weight of his own sin and guilt. The broken relationship with God dominated his thinking. He realized that his only hope lay in God's mercy. **Lovingkindness** is the important Hebrew word *hesed.* The word refers to the quality of God's love based on His covenant with His people. The word can be translated "unfailing love" (NIV) or "steadfast love" (NRSV). How did David know that God had such love? In our day we look back to the cross. In David's day the clearest statement of divine love for sinners was in Exodus 34:6-7. Although David did not quote these verses, he seemed to have had them in mind. **Multitude of thy tender mercies** ("the greatness of Your compassion," NASB) is the third way David referred to the character of the One from whom he sought forgiveness.

David used three words to describe the wrongdoing for which he needed forgiveness. **Transgressions** *(pesa')* contains the idea of stubborn refusal. The word was used to describe the rebellion of a subject against a king. Transgression is refusal to obey God. It is conscious rebellion against the God of love by deliberately breaking His commandments. **Iniquity** *('awon)* refers to perverting God's will and way. This is sin's power to twist and turn someone from God. It underscores the blackness of sin, the perversion of right, and the depravity of such conduct. **Sin** *(hatta't)* refers to missing the mark of what God wants one to be. All three words are in Exodus 34:6-7. David used all three terms to depict the evil he had done.

David also used three ways of describing how he wanted God to deal with his sins. **Blot out** refers to removing his sin. (See the "Word Study.") **Wash me thoroughly** *(kabas)* refers to the kind of washing of dirty clothes used in that time, when clothes were rubbed and pounded on the rocks beside a stream. David wanted a total cleansing. **Cleanse** *(taher)* is a word used to describe the declaration by a priest that a leper had been cleansed. Thus David saw himself as a moral and spiritual leper, one who wanted the Lord to cleanse him and then declare him clean.

The first two verses remind us what is involved in forgiveness—divine or human. It is the removal of some hurt inflicted on another person or on God. Forgiveness in human situations occurs when the person who was hurt absorbs the hurt and offers fellowship to the guilty party. When God forgives a sinner, He absorbs the hurt of the sin and removes it as a barrier to fellowship with Him.

What are the lasting truths of these verses?

1. God's love is the basis for a sinner's hope for forgiveness.
2. Sin is rebellion, perversion, and failing to do God's will.
3. Forgiveness is possible when the barrier to fellowship is removed.

Many people have confused ideas about God, sin, and forgiveness. Here are some examples. How do verses 1-2 speak to each of these?

1. "If there is a God, He is not concerned about me and what I do."

_____

2. "Sin is an out-dated, old-fashioned idea."

_____

Acknowledge Guilt (Ps. 51:3-6)

What shows that David acknowledged the guilt of his sin? What shows that all sin is against God? Why did David not mention his sins against Bathsheba and Uriah? What is the meaning of verse 5?

Verses 3-4: For I acknowledge my transgressions: and my sin is ever before me. ⁴Against thee, thee only, have I sinned, and done this evil in thy sight: that thou mightest be justified when thou speakest, and be clear when thou judgest.

David went for many months without confessing his sin; then he was brought to the point where he had to **acknowledge** his **transgressions.** He confessed his sins to God. During the months of silence, David had tried to hide his sins from God and from others and to not think of his guilt. However, he was forced to see that his **sin** was **ever before** him. Notice in verses 1-3 the use of **I . . . my . . . me**—words that show David confessing that this was his sin and that he was guilty of it.

Verse 4 shows that David recognized the seriousness of his sin because all sin is ultimately against God. Many people have wondered how David could say, **Against thee, thee only, have I sinned, and done this evil in thy sight.** They wonder why David did not acknowledge the terrible sins he had committed against Bathsheba and Uriah. It was not because David was unaware of his sins against these two—and against others. David knew that, at its heart, sin ultimately is against God Himself. This is what makes sin so serious. It is sin against God.

The last part of verse 4 shows that David considered God was totally just and fair in however He dealt with him: "So it is right and fair for you to correct and punish me" (CEV).

Verses 5-6: **Behold, I was shapen in iniquity; and in sin did my mother conceive me. [6]Behold, thou desirest truth in the inward parts: and in the hidden part thou shalt make me to know wisdom.**

Verse 5 is another difficult verse to understand. It has been the basis for many interpretations. Some have said this verse means that David was illegitimate. Others see it as evidence that sex, even within marriage, is sinful. Others have found support for the doctrine of inherited sin and guilt in this verse. The Bible teaches that we inherit a world of sin and a nature turned in that direction. Because we are born into a sinful world with a nature inclined toward sin, at some point all of us commit the basic sin of turning aside from God into our own ways. *The Baptist Faith and Message (2000),* Article III, "Man," states in part: "Through the temptation of Satan man transgressed the command of God, and fell from his original innocence whereby his posterity inherit a nature and an environment inclined toward sin. Therefore, as soon as they are capable of moral action, they become transgressors and are under condemnation." Artur Weiser commented: "It is the tragedy of man that he is born into a world full of sin. The environment in which a child grows up is already saturated with sin and temptation; and when the child learns to distinguish between good and evil he discovers already in himself a natural tendency of his own will that is at variance with the will of God."[1]

We sometimes speak of an age of accountability. This is the age at which a child or youth becomes convicted that the wrong he or she does is sin against God. Children generally learn the difference between right and wrong early in life, but they do not associate wrong with sin until they are mature enough to have a sense of God and His expectations. In other words, a child may realize early that it is wrong to disobey his parents; but he becomes morally accountable when he sees his disobeying as sin against God.

Verse 6 shows that God wants honest and truthful hearts and lives: "But you want complete honesty, so teach me true wisdom" (CEV).

What are the lasting truths in these verses?

1. When guilty sinners honestly face their sins, they confess them to God.
2. All sin is ultimately against God.
3. We are born into a sinful world with natures inclined toward sin, but we become guilty of sin when we become morally accountable.

People have some confused ideas about the confession of sin. How do verses 3-6 help to answer these confusions?

1. "I know I've made some mistakes—some of them pretty serious. But what good will forgiveness do? Why cry over spilled milk? I'll just try harder in the future."

_____

2. "If you knew my parents and how I was raised, you wouldn't hold my sins against me."

_____

3. "If I choose to do wrong, I'm hurting no one but myself."

_____

4. "I don't worry about committing some sin. I know I always can go to God and confess my sin. When I do, He will forgive me."

_____

Pray for Renewal (Ps. 51:7-12)

What do these verses add to verses 1-2 about being forgiven? What do they reveal about David's experience while he did not confess his sins? What are the results of sins being forgiven?

Verses 7-12: Purge me with hyssop, and I shall be clean: wash me, and I shall be whiter than snow. [8]Make me to hear joy and gladness; that the bones which thou hast broken may rejoice. [9]Hide thy face from my sins, and blot out all mine iniquities. [10]Create in me a clean heart, O God; and renew a right spirit within me. [11]Cast me not away from thy presence; and take not thy holy spirit from me. [12]Restore unto me the joy of thy salvation; and uphold me with thy free spirit.

These verses repeat some of the words used in verses 1-2. **Blot out** and **wash** are in both passages. These verses also add some new words about what happens in forgiveness.

Hyssop was a plant used in the ceremonial cleansing of lepers (Lev. 14:1-5) and of people who had contact with dead bodies (Num. 19:18). David rightly saw himself as a moral leper whose sin had made him unclean and unacceptable to God. He asked for this defilement to be purged away.

Wash is the same word used in verse 2, but the words **whiter than snow** are new in this psalm. Convicted sinners feel dirty and unclean. God promises, "Though your sins be as scarlet, they shall be as white as snow" (Isa. 1:18). **Hide thy face from my sins** suggests removing sin as a barrier to fellowship with God. A newly forgiven sinner feels cleansed and renewed.

Verses 7-12 provide insight into David's experience during the months when he tried to hide his sin and did not confess it to the Lord. Several references in verses 7-12 refer to the absence of **joy.** Other references refer to David's sense of the loss of God's loving and abiding presence. True believers who try to live with unconfessed sin do not lose their salvation, but they do lose the joy of God's salvation and the sense of God's approving presence. When David was trying to hide his sins, he was miserable. Verse 8 reflects that period in David's spiritual pilgrimage. He prayed for a renewal of **joy and gladness.** In verse 12 he pleaded with the Lord, **Restore unto me the joy of thy salvation.** David wrote of **the bones which** God had **broken. Bones** in the Old Testament sometimes refers to the literal bones in our bodies. At other times, the word is used metaphorically for the sense of inward distress. In Psalm 32:3 David wrote, "When I kept silence, my bones waxed old through my roaring all the day long."

David asked God to **hide** his **face from** his **sins.** But he asked God not to hide Himself from David: **Cast me not away from thy presence; and take not thy holy spirit from me.** Perhaps David was thinking of the sad case of King Saul, from whom the Lord withdrew His Spirit (1 Sam. 16:1,7). David, the man after God's own heart, could not imagine anything so terrible; however, during the long months of his unconfessed sin, he had a taste of what that would be like.

If people can commit sins without feeling miserable and lost, they are in greater peril than those who miss the presence of God in their lives. For a person such as David, he missed his chief source of joy—the assurance of the Lord's presence and favor. This shows that he was a true believer. His very misery helped him return to the Lord.

Verse 10 is a good summary verse for the heart of David's prayer. The word **create** is the same word used in Genesis 1 for God's creation of all things out of nothing *(bara).* Thus David was praying that God would make him a new creation (see 2 Cor. 5:17). This new creation would have a **clean heart.** He was asking for a new nature different from his old sinful nature. David's experience was also a renewal of what he had known in the past, although now his experience would be enhanced. **Renew a right** ("steadfast," NKJV) **spirit within me.** If the first part of verse 10 is parallel to 2 Corinthians 5:17, the last part is parallel to 2 Corinthians 4:16. We are new creations in Christ, but we are being "renewed day by day." Living for the Lord takes a renewal of our relationship with the Lord. I've found it helpful to add Psalm 51:10 to my daily prayers. I need to have the Lord continue to keep renewing a right spirit within me. Only in the Lord's strength can we live life as it is intended to be lived. Only the assurance of His presence and help can enable us to do this.

David thus sought and no doubt found many good results of confessing his sins. He escaped the misery of loss of joy and close fellowship with the Lord. He found a renewed sense of forgiveness, the closeness of God's presence, and the renewed joy of salvation. We know from reading the last part of 1 Samuel that although God forgave David's sins, David spent the last part of his life reaping the earthly consequences of his sins, just as Nathan had predicted. Thus forgiveness renews us in the Lord, but we continue to reap the bitter harvest of some things that cannot be changed.

What are the lasting truths in these verses?

1. Unconfessed sin in a believer's life can rob the believer of the joy that comes from a sense of God's presence.

2. When sin is forgiven, God removes the guilt of our sin, restores the sense of His presence, and renews the joy of our salvation.

3. Although God forgives the guilt of our sin when we repent, some of sin's consequences cannot be changed.

Here are some confused ideas people have about the results of confessing sin. How do verses 7-12 speak to each of these ideas?

1. "I've asked God to forgive me, but I still feel guilty."

_____

2. "I've sought forgiveness and have found it, but I can't seem to stop returning to one particular sin."

_____

3. "I was forgiven once for all when I was saved. Why do I need to keep asking God to forgive my sins?"

_____

4. "I am a professing Christian, but I feel miserable and have no sense of the Lord's presence with me."

_____

Commit to Serve (Ps. 51:13-17)

*What commitment did David make as a result of being forgiven? How serious was the sin of **bloodguiltiness**? What did David say about praising the Lord? What did he say was more important than the sacrificial system?*

Verses 13-17: Then will I teach transgressors thy ways; and sinners shall be converted unto thee. [14]Deliver me from blood-guiltiness, O God, thou God of my salvation: and my tongue shall sing aloud of thy righteousness. [15]O Lord, open thou my lips; and my mouth shall show forth thy praise. [16]For thou desirest not sacrifice; else would I give it: thou delightest not in burnt offering. [17]The sacrifices of God are a broken spirit: a broken and a contrite heart, O God, thou wilt not despise.

David announced his commitment to help others who were living in sin. He promised God to **teach transgressors** the Lord's **ways.** The result would be that **sinners** would **be converted** to the Lord. This is the normal way for a forgiven sinner to feel and the normal commitment to make. We who have received God's salvation are debtors to tell others who need it the good news (Rom. 1:14-16). Something is wrong with the experience of professed believers who lack such a commitment.

Toward the end of the psalm, David asked God to forgive him from his worst sin against others. **Bloodguiltiness** was used in the Old Testament to describe several ways in which one person took the life of another. By far the most serious of these was the kind of sin David had committed—the premeditated murder of an innocent person. This is what David had done with Uriah. David's sin with Bathsheba may have been impulsive. This doesn't excuse it at all; however, his sin against Uriah was cold, calculated murder. It did not matter that he did not hold the weapon that took the life of this loyal soldier. David was the murderer as much as if he had personally killed Uriah.

The blood of such innocent victims cried out to God for vengeance (Gen. 4:10). The community acting in the name of God was to put to death anyone guilty of this crime (Num. 35:33). Under the Jewish law, the sacrificial system offered help only for certain kinds of sins. For sins committed with a high hand—especially bloodguilt—the sacrificial system offered no recourse (15:27-31). God Himself, through a special act of His mercy, could forgive someone of such a sin. The God whose Son later died for all the sins of all the sinners forgave David.

David asked the Lord not only to let him speak words that God would use to convert sinners, but he also asked the Lord to **open** his **lips** and his **mouth** so he might **praise** the Lord. Remember David was a singer and poet. After a long, dry period of his life, he wanted to again praise the Lord with words and songs. He could do this only when he was forgiven and restored.

Referring to verse 16, H. C. Leupold wrote: "This is one of the statements of deepest spiritual insight found in the whole of the Old Testament. It is akin to Is. 57:15. A pardoned sinner alone knows what it means. It is not a disparagement of sacrifices that are offered after the pattern of the Mosaic ritual. But it does indicate what true spiritual sacrifices are."[2] David obviously was not declaring that the sacrificial system was no good. After all, he wanted to build a temple in which such sacrifices would be offered. David was ahead of his time. The prophets later condemned trusting sacrifices and formal worship when the people's hearts and lives were sinful. Isaiah said that some who came to worship even had hands full of blood (Isa. 1:15). True worship is truly meeting with the Lord and going forth to live for Him. The beginning point for this is **a broken spirit: a broken and a contrite heart.** David could have offered all kinds of animal sacrifices, but he knew that forgiveness comes when a sinner's heart is broken by the heavy weight of his sin and guilt and he turns to God for mercy. Only then does God forgive someone's sins.

What are the lasting truths in these verses?

1. When people are forgiven of their sins, they want to tell others of God's saving grace.

2. God can forgive even the worst of our sins.

3. Witness and worship are results of experiencing God's forgiveness.

4. No amount of formal worship can substitute for the godly sorrow in true repentance.

People have confused ideas about many of the truths in these verses. Based on these verses, what would you say to each kind of confused person?

1. "I'm no preacher. I feel no need to try to convert others. After all, what would the guys at work say if I started preaching to them?"

---

2. "You don't realize how terrible my sin is. It's too great to be forgiven."

---

3. "I go to church regularly. Isn't that enough?"

❖ *Spiritual Transformations*

David's prayer for forgiveness began with the source of his hope for forgiveness—God's mercy. David confessed the seriousness of his sins. He prayed for the renewal of his sense of the Lord's presence and the joy that went with it. He committed himself to words of worship and witness based on his broken heart caused by his sin.

The *Life Question* this lesson seeks to address is, "How can I experience God's forgiveness after I've sinned?" This reminds me of a book for golfers. On the cover is the title, "How to Get Out of the Rough." (For you non-golfers, the rough is the high grass beside the fairway.) Inside the book is this one piece of advice, "Don't get in it." As believers, our goal should be to avoid sin at all costs. However, Jesus taught us to pray, "Forgive us our sins" (Luke 11:4). He knew that His followers would not be perfect. Hopefully few believers commit sins as serious as David's sins were, but even the best Christians have sins of omission and sins of the spirit. The lasting truths of this lesson apply to all kinds of sins in the lives of believers.

Which of the lasting truths in this lesson speaks most to you?

All of us know people who are confused about God, about sin, and about forgiveness. Who do you know who needs help in understanding the truths from Psalm 51? _____

Prayer of Commitment: God, be merciful to me, a sinner. Forgive my sins. Renew a right spirit within me. Help me to live and speak so others will come to know You and Your great love. Amen.

[1]Artur Weiser, *The Psalms*, in The Old Testament Library [Philadelphia: The Westminster Press, 1962], 405.
[2]Leupold, *Exposition of the Psalms*, 407.

Week of September 29

GOD PROVIDES

Background Passage: 1 Kings 17:1-24; 19:1-18
Focal Passage: 1 Kings 17:1-4; 19:9b-18
Key Verse: 1 Kings 17:4

❖ *Significance of the Lesson*

• The *Theme* of this lesson is that God provides for His people.
• The *Life Question* this lesson seeks to address is, How does God provide for me?
• The *Biblical Truth* is that God's provision for His people includes physical sustenance, assurance of His presence, and watchcare over His purpose and plan for His people.
• The *Life Impact* is to help you depend on God who provides.

Do People Need What God Can Provide?

In a secular worldview, the answer to the question "Do people need what God can provide?" is no. The definition of secularism is humanity's ability to get along without God. Secular people often pride themselves on their independence and self-sufficiency. Dependence on God is regarded as a "crutch" needed only by weak people.

In the biblical worldview, we live and move and have our being in God. He can be trusted to supply all we need to do what He wants us to do. He meets our basic physical needs, assures us of His presence, and enables us to help do our part in His purpose and plan.

Word Study: *left*

The English word *left* is found several times in 1 Kings 19. This one English word is used to translate several different Hebrew words. The most significant of these Hebrew words for this lesson is in verse 18. This is the word *sa'ar,* which means "left behind." The word can be translated "will leave" (NASB, NRSV, NEB), "reserve" (NIV), and "have reserved" (NKJV). Verse 18 refers to 7,000 Israelites who would not bow their knees to Baal. This was in response to Elijah's complaint that he was the only one left who remained faithful to God.

❖ *Search the Scriptures*

Elijah announced to Israel's King Ahab that no rain would fall in Israel except by the prophet's word. The Lord led Elijah into the wilderness where He fed him using ravens. After a tremendous victory by Elijah for the Lord on Mount Carmel, Elijah fled to the south and asked that he might die. The Lord fed him and then at Mount Horeb revealed Himself to Elijah with a still small voice. Then the Lord gave the prophet three things to do and assured him that 7,000 others had not bowed their knees to Baal.

From this lesson we learn three ways God provides for His people.

God Meets Physical Needs (1 Kings 17:1-4)

*Who was Elijah? What crisis was Israel facing? What part did Ahab play in the ministry of Elijah? What is the significance of the words **before whom I stand**? Why did Elijah pray for a drought? What words in verse 2 are used for most Old Testament prophets? Why did the Lord send Elijah into the wilderness? How did God feed the prophet?*

17:1: And Elijah the Tishbite, who was of the inhabitants of Gilead, said unto Ahab, As the LORD God of Israel liveth, before whom I stand, there shall not be dew nor rain these years, but according to my word.

The name **Elijah** means "The LORD is God." This was an appropriate name for a prophet who would stand for this truth in a critical time in Israel's history. We are not told anything about Elijah prior to this verse. We know nothing of his family. We are not even sure where Tishbe was located. We do not have anything he wrote. Elijah suddenly appeared unannounced.

He lived in the time of Israel's King **Ahab,** whose sordid history is summarized in 16:29-34: "Ahab the son of Omri did evil in the sight of the LORD above all that were before him" (v. 30). Ahab opened the door to the worst spiritual crisis faced by Israel up to that time. He married Jezebel, a princess from Sidon in Phoenicia, and a fervent worshiper of Baal. Ahab not only built her a temple for her worship but also gave her a free hand in seeking to replace the worship of the Lord with Baal worship. First Kings 18:4 shows she killed God's prophets. Baal worship was the native religion of many people in the Near East, and it had been a threat to Israel since they first came in contact with it. However, this was the first time that one of the kings of Israel had persecuted followers of the Lord and made Baal the official god of the royal house.

Baal worship was attractive to the Israelites for several reasons. Among these reasons were that it was a fertility religion that used temple prostitutes in its worship rituals and that it promised rain and good crops. When the Israelites came into Canaan, they knew little about farming; thus, they naturally asked advice from the Canaanite farmers. They told the Israelites that worshiping Baal was the key to success in raising crops in this land. The promise of rain was the basis for the drought that Elijah called down on Israel.

Elijah was a man of prayer. Although Elijah was as human as anyone else, his prayers closed the heavens to rain for three-and-one-half years. Then he prayed and the rains came (Jas. 5:16-18). He did this through prayer and in accordance with the Lord's will. The purpose was to show the people that Baal did not send the rain—the Lord did.

One of the most intriguing parts of Elijah's work was a series of confrontations with King Ahab. There were at least four: (1) when Elijah told Ahab of the drought (17:1), (2) when Elijah returned to Israel and challenged the Baal prophets to a contest to prove who was God (18:16-19), (3) at the contest on Mount Carmel (vv. 41-45), and (4) when Elijah pronounced doom to Ahab and Jezebel for the murder of Naboth (21:17-24).

To confront the king, Elijah had to be endued with God's word. The words **before whom I stand** ("whom I serve," NIV) imply a close confidential official position. Because Elijah stood before the Lord as a faithful prophet, the Lord empowered him to speak His word boldly.

17:2-4: And the word of the Lord came unto him, saying, ³Get thee hence, and turn thee eastward, and hide thyself by the brook Cherith, that is before Jordan. ⁴And it shall be, that thou shalt drink of the brook; and I have commanded the ravens to feed thee there.

The words **and the word of the Lord came unto him** remind us that the prophets did not speak on their own initiative nor did they deliver their own messages. Their message was their power, and it was **the word of the Lord.** The Lord also spoke to each prophet and told him what he was to do. In these verses the Lord told Elijah to leave where he was and go to a place designated by God. When word got around that Elijah had prayed for the drought, Ahab would not be the only one seeking his life.

The exact location of **the brook Cherith** is debated. Most translators place it "east of the Jordan" (v. 5, NIV). Wherever it was, it was where Ahab could not get his hands on Elijah for a while. During his time there, Elijah was dependent on the Lord for basic provisions. The brook, which was still flowing at this time, provided water. The Lord **commanded the ravens to feed** him. The ravens obeyed and brought him bread and meat in the morning and in the evening (v. 6). This is an evidence of the providence of God—His provision of food for His people. When the brook dried up, the Lord led the prophet to Zarephath outside of Israel. God used the generosity of a poor widow to feed the hungry prophet. As a reward for her sacrifice, the Lord caused her jar of oil and her barrel of flour to remain full (vv. 8-16). God uses various ways to provide for the needs of His faithful servants. Later, when Elijah fled into the wilderness, the Lord sent an angel to feed him (19:5-8).

God's promise to His servants is that He will supply what they need to do His will. Jesus taught us to pray for daily bread (Matt. 6:11), knowing that all food ultimately is from the Lord. This includes the food we grow or purchase with money. The point is that people of faith trust the Lord to supply what they need to do His will.

> Be not dismayed whate'er betide,
> God will take care of you;
> Beneath His wings of love abide,
> God will take care of you.
> God will take care of you,
> Through ev'ry day, o'er all the way;
> He will take care of you,
> God will take care of you.[1]

What lasting truths are in these verses?

1. In working out His good purpose, God calls gifted people to do His work.

2. God supplies the needs of His servants as they do His will.

3. God and His servants maintain touch through prayer.

God Sustains with His Presence (1 Kings 19:9b-14)

*What happened in 1 Kings 18:1–19:9a? Why did the Lord ask Elijah the question, **What doest thou here?** What does Elijah's answer reveal* *about his current attitude toward others, himself, and God? Why was God not in the **wind . . . earthquake . . . fire**? What lessons was God trying to teach Elijah by speaking to him in **a still small voice**?*

19:9b-10: Behold, the word of the LORD came to him, and he said unto him, What doest thou here, Elijah? **¹⁰**And he said, I have been very jealous for the LORD God of hosts: for the children of Israel have forsaken thy covenant, thrown down thine altars, and slain thy prophets with the sword; and I, even I only, am left; and they seek my life, to take it away.

The contest with the prophets of Baal was the central feature of 1 Kings 18. Also Elijah prayed for rain, and the rains came. He felt the Lord had clearly shown that He alone was God. Elijah had focused his hopes on this event. He expected it to signal the downfall of the evil system of Jezebel and her followers. Yet when he ran down the mountain, he heard that Jezebel had threatened to kill him by the next day. Elijah was no coward, but this news shattered his confidence; and he fled from the north of Israel beyond the south of Judah. Leaving his servant, he plunged farther into the desert. Falling down at a juniper tree, he prayed that the Lord would take his life. Instead, the Lord sent an angel to feed him and give him sleep. When he had his strength back, he went to Mount Horeb, another name for Mount Sinai, and lodged in a cave. He was there when the Lord asked him, **What doest thou here, Elijah** ("What are you doing here, Elijah?" NKJV)?

Verse 10 records Elijah's long answer, which was basically an attempt to justify his actions in running away. His words reveal how he viewed others, himself, and God at this spiritually low point in his life. He was very disappointed and angry with the people of Israel. He had such high hopes for them. On Mount Carmel they at first were unwilling to commit themselves (18:21), but after the Lord sent fire from heaven, they enthusiastically declared that the Lord was God (v. 39). But after he received Jezebel's threat, Elijah realized that the people would not stand against the evil queen or risk themselves for the Lord and His prophet. Thus he accused the people (not just Jezebel and her fanatical followers) of forsaking the Lord's **covenant,** throwing **down** His **altars,** and slaying His **prophets.**

The disgruntled prophet saw himself as the only one who was faithful to the Lord. His vision at this point was egocentric and filled with self-pity. The word **jealous** refers to ardent service for the Lord. He added, **I, even I only, am left.** The prophet had a distorted view of others and of himself. Nothing explicit is said of God, but what is implied in the words **and they seek my life, to take it away**? Don't these words imply that he no longer trusted God to take care of him?

19:11-14: **And he said, Go forth, and stand upon the mount before the Lᴏʀᴅ. And, behold, the Lᴏʀᴅ passed by, and a great and strong wind rent the mountains, and brake in pieces the rocks before the Lᴏʀᴅ; but the Lᴏʀᴅ was not in the wind: and after the wind an earthquake; but the Lᴏʀᴅ was not in the earthquake:** [12]**and after the earthquake a fire; but the Lᴏʀᴅ was not in the fire: and after the fire a still small voice.** [13]**And it was so, when Elijah heard it, that he wrapped his face in his mantle, and went out, and stood in the entering in of the cave. And, behold, there came a voice unto him, and said, What doest thou here, Elijah?** [14]**And he said, I have been very jealous for the Lᴏʀᴅ God of hosts: because the children of Israel have forsaken thy covenant, thrown down thine altars, and slain thy prophets with the sword; and I, even I only, am left; and they seek my life, to take it away.**

The first part of verse 11 reminds us of Exodus 33:18-23. While Moses was interceding with the Lord to forgive the Israelites after the golden calf incident, he asked to see God's glory. The Lord told him that no one could see God's face and live. However, the Lord agreed to tell Moses His name. The Lord hid Moses in a cleft of the rock and covered him there with His hand. Moses was not allowed to see God coming, but he did see Him after He passed by. In 1 Kings 19:11 the Lord called Elijah **to stand upon the mount before the Lᴏʀᴅ.**

As **the Lᴏʀᴅ passed by . . . a great and strong wind rent the mountains, and brake in pieces the rocks before the Lᴏʀᴅ.** On other occasions, the Lord revealed Himself in a mighty wind. He spoke to Job out of a whirlwind (Job 38:1). However, this time, **the Lᴏʀᴅ was not in the wind: and after the wind an earthquake.** At other times, the Lord revealed Himself in an earthquake. He did this, for example, before giving the Ten Commandments to Israel (Ex. 19:18). However, this time, **the Lᴏʀᴅ was not in the earthquake.** Then the Lord sent **a fire; but the Lᴏʀᴅ was not in the fire.** He had been in the fire on Mount Carmel but not in this distinctive revelation to Elijah.

Last of all, in the silence following the noise of the wind, earthquake, and fire, the Lord spoke to the prophet in **a still small voice** ("a gentle whisper," NIV; "a sound of sheer silence," NRSV; "a sound of a gentle blowing," NASB). God obviously was trying to teach something to the discouraged prophet. In effect, He was saying to Elijah: "Let Me be God. I've been doing this for a long time, and I know what I'm doing. I may not do things the way you want or expect. Let Me do things My way, and in My own time and method. You expected evil to be destroyed in one day with fire from heaven, but evil must be destroyed within the human heart where it resides. My word is still your mighty sword." We prefer quick fixes to problems, but God must defeat evil in His own way and in His own time.

Overall, verses 9b-14 represent an attempt by God to reassure the prophet of His abiding presence. He was present not always as Elijah expected or desired, but He was present nonetheless.

> I need Thy presence ev'ry passing hour;
> What but Thy grace can foil the tempter's pow'r?
> Who like Thyself my guide and stay can be?
> Thro' cloud and sunshine, O abide with me![2]

What lasting truths are in these verses?

1. God deals with discouraged servants gently but firmly.

2. When a servant is discouraged, the servant often is impatient with others, filled with self-pity, and weak in trust in the Lord.

3. God is God, and His servants must learn to trust Him to do His work in His own way and in His own time.

4. God seeks to reassure His servants of His abiding presence as the most important of His provisions for their needs.

God Gives Purpose for Living (1 Kings 19:15-18)

What shows that Elijah thought his life and ministry were over? How did God show him that he still had God's work to do? Why did God tell him of the 7,000 who had not bowed the knee to Baal? How is a sense of God's purpose essential to faithful service?

19:15-17: And the LORD said unto him, Go, return on thy way to the wilderness of Damascus: and when thou comest, anoint Hazael to be king over Syria: [16]and Jehu the son of Nimshi shalt thou anoint to be king over Israel: and Elisha the son of Shaphat of Abel‑meholah shalt thou anoint to be prophet in thy room. [17]And it shall come to pass, that him that escapeth the sword of Hazael shall Jehu slay: and him that escapeth from the sword of Jehu shall Elisha slay.

Elijah seems to have thought that his ministry and life were over. Leaving his servant behind is one clue to his feeling about his ministry (v. 3). At the foot of the juniper tree, he asked God to take his life (v. 4). At Mount Horeb, he twice said that the people were intent on killing him (vv. 10,14). Like many of God's servants during times of discouragement, Elijah felt that God had nothing left for him to do.

This is a deadly attitude to faithful service. Of course, at some point each servant's ministry and life comes to an end; however, we ought to leave that in God's hand and not make assumptions of our own. We need to be ready to live and serve as long as the Lord allows, and we need to be ready to go to be with Him.

God showed that He still had work for Elijah to do. He told him, **Go, return on thy way** ("Go back the way you came," NIV). Then He gave Elijah three specific tasks. Elijah was to go into the foreign land of Syria and **anoint Hazael to be king over Syria.** He also was to anoint **Jehu . . . to be king over Israel.** Finally, and most important, he was to anoint **Elisha . . . to be prophet in thy room** ("place," NKJV). The account of Elijah's anointing Elisha is recorded in verses 19-21. All three of these people were to play key roles in God's judgment on Ahab and Jezebel and their family. Verse 17 makes this plain.

***19:18:* Yet I have left me seven thousand in Israel, all the knees which have not bowed unto Baal, and every mouth which hath not kissed him.**

The Lord's final words at Mount Horeb were designed to deal with Elijah's self-pity and sense of being the only one who was faithful to God. The Lord told the prophet that he was wrong about being the only one left. **Seven thousand** others had **not bowed unto Baal.** As we saw in the "Word Study," **left** refers to a faithful remnant who were true to the Lord. Wouldn't it have been great for Elijah to have spent some time with some of these? Then he would not have felt so alone in his service to the Lord. Believers are always a part of a vast host of people who love and serve the Lord. This is one of the main purposes for the church and its Bible study classes. Through being together, praying together, and studying God's Word together, each person's faith is strengthened. Believers who try to go it alone often feel overwhelmed by the vast number of unbelievers.

The words of verses 15-18 were designed to renew Elijah's sense of purpose. He had a purpose within the larger purpose of the Lord. He could not do the tasks of others, but he was accountable for doing what God called him to do.

A number of years ago Vance Havner spoke to a pastor's conference. He used the word *resign* in three different ways to show three options for people who serve the Lord. He said that people can resign in the sense of giving up. People can continue to serve but resign themselves to do so reluctantly. Or people can "re-sign" their commitment to serve. That is, they can renew their commitment to serve the Lord in His strength for as long as He gives us time and strength to do so.

What lasting truths are in these verses?

1. God's servants need to have their sense of calling and purpose renewed from time to time.

2. We should leave in God's hand the time and manner of the end of our ministries and of our lives.

3. We should use what strength and days we have to do what the Lord wants us to do.

4. We should encourage one another to fulfill God's larger purpose by each doing his or her specific task.

❖ *Spiritual Transformations*

Three aspects of how God provides for His people are provisions, presence, and purpose. The Lord provided physical provisions for Elijah. He reassured Elijah of His presence at a low point in the prophet's life. He renewed Elijah's sense of divine purpose for his life.

Evaluate your actions and attitudes in light of these aspects of God's provision. With which of these do you most identify?

Do you need to trust the Lord to provide for your physical needs?

_____

*Do you need to be reassured of the Lord's presence with you?*____

_____

Do you need to renew your commitment to God's purpose for your life? _____

Prayer of Commitment: Lord, help me to trust You to provide for my needs, to know Your abiding presence, and to fulfill Your purpose for my life. Amen.

[1]Civilla D. Martin, "God Will Take Care of You," No. 64, *The Baptist Hymnal,* 1991.
[2]Henry F. Lyte, "Abide with Me," No. 63, *The Baptist Hymnal,* 1991.

Study Theme

Covenants of Grace

The covenants of the Old Testament provide a summary of the phases of God's redemptive plan during those years. In this study we will look at the four key Old Testament covenants. In each case, God initiated the covenant. In each case, the covenant was given to one person, but its ultimate fulfillment included many others.

The covenant in the first lesson, "Committing to Life," God made with Noah. This was an unconditional covenant. Although spoken to Noah, this covenant was actually a promise to all human and animal life that God would never again destroy the earth by a flood. God gave the rainbow as a sign of His promise.

The covenant in the second lesson, "Blessing All Nations," God made with Abraham. The emphasis is on the promise to bless all nations through Abraham. The covenant with Abraham ultimately applied to all people of faith like that of Abraham's. This lesson has a missionary application.

The covenant in the third lesson, "Creating a Distinctive People," God gave to Moses. The covenant with Moses was actually through Moses to all Israel. This was a conditional covenant calling for Israel to obey God's commandments. The Ten Commandments are the main Bible verses in this lesson.

The covenant in the fourth lesson, "Promising a Righteous Ruler," God made with David. The covenant with David also extended in time and application far beyond David's time. This unconditional covenant—like the covenants with Abraham and Moses—was ultimately fulfilled in Jesus Christ.

Each of these four lessons is designed to have a life impact on those who study it. The four lessons are designed to help you—

• build a biblically based view about the value and future of life (Oct. 6)

• extend God's blessing by helping all people have an opportunity to know the one, true God (Oct. 13)

• live in full obedience to God's law (Oct. 20)

• live under the authority of God's righteous Ruler (Oct. 27)

COMMITTING TO LIFE

Background Passage: Genesis 8:20–9:17
Focal Passage: Genesis 9:1-6,8-17
Key Verses: Genesis 9:14-15

❖ *Significance of the Lesson*

• The *Theme* of this lesson is that God's covenant relationship with Noah included that God would never again destroy all life by flooding the whole earth.

• The *Life Question* this lesson seeks to address is, How can I have hope about life when so much seems wrong?

• The *Biblical Truth* is that God revealed to Noah His covenant to preserve and redeem His creation rather than to destroy it.

• The *Life Impact* is to help you build a biblically based view about the value and future of life.

Value of Human Life

In the secular worldview, human life is not always considered precious. Life is often seen as a purely natural phenomenon. Ending life, therefore, is not always viewed in the same way as it is by those who hold the biblical view. Genocide is the worst example of a secular view, although many people abhor it. Some secular people condone abortion and euthanasia. Violence is widespread. Most people value their own lives and those of their friends and family, and they fear for their lives in an increasingly violent society.

In the biblical worldview, human life is seen as the creation and gift of God. He is committed to creating new life and to preserving, sustaining, and redeeming life. God expects His people to place high value on life.

Word Study: *Covenant*

The Hebrew word for **covenant** is *berith*. It is found seven times in the Focal Passage. Old Testament examples of covenants include covenants between humans and between God and humans. Covenants were of two kinds: those between equals and those in which one of the parties was superior. In covenants of God with humans, God always takes the initiative and is always the One of greater authority. These covenants included promises by God. Some of His covenants were conditional and some were unconditional. Even the unconditional covenants had expectations for human behavior.

❖ *Search the Scriptures*

After the flood, God made a covenant with Noah and through him with all living beings. In the new start, God repeated the command to be co-creators of new human life. He made provision for food. He warned against taking human life, and He warned that He would hold accountable anyone who committed murder. God based this on a reaffirmation of humans being in His image. He established His covenant with all living beings, promising never again to destroy the earth by flood. And He gave the rainbow as a sign that He would remember this covenant promise.

As you study this passage, look for the answers to these two questions: (1) What shows God's commitment to life? (2) What shows the commitment of humans to life?

New Start; Clear Accountability (Gen. 9:1-6)

How and why did God offer humanity a new start? What parts of God's original good creation were still intact after the flood? What is the significance of repeating Genesis 1:28 after the flood? What provision for food did God make? What prohibition did God make about eating meat? How should humans treat animals? How does verse 5 answer Cain's question, "Am I my brother's keeper?" What does verse 6 teach or imply about murder, capital punishment, revenge, and the state?

Verse 1: And God blessed Noah and his sons, and said unto them, Be fruitful, and multiply, and replenish the earth.

God made a new start with **Noah and his sons.** The **sons** were crucial in this because of their children and their descendants. God **blessed** them by repeating to them part of the commission of 1:28: **Be fruitful, and multiply, and replenish the earth** ("Be fruitful and increase in number and fill the earth," NIV). God had begun the human race with Adam and Eve. Now all people, except for Noah and his family, were dead. In a sense, Noah became the new Adam, through whom the human race was to have a new beginning.

Both Genesis 1:28 and 9:1 show several crucial facts about God, man, and new life: (1) God gives new life through human conception and birth; (2) life is the gift of God; (3) human parents are co-creators with God of human life; and (4) children are gifts from God and a trust for parents. The conception and birth of new life is a miracle of God. It was part of the original good creation, and it continued in the covenant with Noah.

Verses 2-4: **And the fear of you and the dread of you shall be upon every beast of the earth, and upon every fowl of the air, upon all that moveth upon the earth, and upon all the fishes of the sea; into your hand are they delivered. [3]Every moving thing that liveth shall be meat for you; even as the green herb have I given you all things. [4]But flesh with the life thereof, which is the blood thereof, shall ye not eat.**

Verse 1 represents something that was part of the original creation, but verses 2-4 represent some changes. In the garden of Eden, before sin came in, Adam and the animals lived together in a harmonious relationship. He named the animals. Prior to the flood nothing explicit is said about humans eating animals. In fact, verse 3 mentions **the green herb** ("green plants," NIV) that God earlier had given man to eat. Now after the flood, however, God told Noah and his sons, **Every moving thing that liveth shall be meat for you.** God told the human survivors that **into your hand they are delivered.** As a result, **every beast** would have **fear** and **dread** of human beings. As a child, I saw the Walt Disney movie *Bambi.* One of the most impressive scenes to a child was the terror the animals shared when they heard that man was in the forest. The death of Bambi's mother brought home this point even more powerfully.

Although humans were allowed to eat the meat of any animal, one strong prohibition was given. No one was allowed to eat **flesh** containing **the blood** of the animal. **The blood** ("lifeblood," NIV) represented the life of the animal. This prohibition became part of the Jewish law. Even in New Testament times, when Gentiles were accepted by faith, James asked that the Gentile converts respect this stipulation because it is not for Jews only but for all humanity (Acts 15:29).

Verses 5-6: *And surely your blood of your lives will I require; at the hand of every beast will I require it, and at the hand of man; at the hand of every man's brother will I require the life of man. ⁶Whoso sheddeth man's blood, by man shall his blood be shed: for in the image of God made he man.*

Moving from the subject of the blood of animals, God turned to the more crucial issue of shedding **man's blood,** the blood of human beings. **Require** has the idea of accountability. The word is used three times in verse 5. In the *New International Version,* **will I require** is translated "I will demand an accounting." Being accountable means to be held responsible by God for one's actions. People and animals that shed innocent human blood will be under divine disfavor and will face judgment if they do not repent.

When God confronted Cain after his murder of Abel, Cain arrogantly denied knowing where Abel was. He asked God, "Am I my brother's keeper?" (4:9). The text there implies the answer, but Genesis 9:5 deals with it head-on: **At the hand of every man's brother will I require the life of a man.** Each person is his brother's keeper.

Verse 6 is even more explicit: **Whoso sheddeth man's blood, by man shall his blood be shed.** This prohibition is based on the fact that, in spite of the coming of sin into the world, humans are still **in the image of God.** Theologians have debated whether sin destroyed or marred **the image of God.** This verse supports the view that although the image is marred by human sin, it is still enough intact for humans to have the potential for a personal relationship with God. Taking the life of someone with this potential is worse than killing an animal.

Verse 6 is an important verse. Even before the Sixth Commandment forbade murder, this verse condemned it. The punishment for premeditated murder must be severe. Most evangelical Bible students see this verse as biblical support for capital punishment for murder. This stipulation assumes that humans would form governments to enforce laws. God was not giving divine sanction to personal vengeance, although in early times retribution was done through a kinsman of the victim. Romans 13:1-7 tells how God instituted the state to maintain law and order and to wield the sword.

How did God show His commitment, and how do we show our commitment, to life?

1. God offered a new start for humanity. In my own lifetime, He has done this several times. In our own personal lives most of us have been given new starts by the Lord. The most important is the new birth, which is not only a new start but also a new life. What new starts has He given you?

2. God gives new life when a child is conceived and born. The birth of a baby is surely a commitment to life.

3. God gives to us the gift of life. Life is a gift and a trust from God to each of us. Life's experiences have a way of reminding us that life is a fragile, precious gift from the Lord. I had a heart attack in October 1990. When I left the hospital following successful treatment for a blocked artery, I felt that God had extended my life and given me a new start. Never was I more aware that life is a fragile, precious gift from God and that I was accountable for how I used my remaining years.

4. God provides us food to eat. We must work for a living, but God puts the food on the table. He provides what we can eat. We are accountable for eating what makes us strong to do the will of God. We pray for daily bread and thank God for providing it.

5. God prohibits murder. We live in a violent world. Many forces interact to take human life unnecessarily. Murders take place in almost every community. Violence sometimes results in gang shootings, terrorist killings, school shootings, and senseless wars. Innocent people are the victims. Other evidences of a callous attitude toward the value of human life are abortions on demand, suicides, accidents caused by alcohol or other drugs, and so-called mercy killings. God made humans accountable for the sin and crime of taking a human life. He expects us to cherish and protect human life.

6. God ordained the state to protect people and to punish criminals. One of my sons is an attorney who works with the district attorney for our county. Based on what Paul wrote in Romans 13, I told my son that he is a minister of God. We may not think of the government as a gift of God and an evidence of His commitment to life, but it is.

Commitment to Preserve Life (Gen. 9:8-11)

Why does God always take the initiative in offering covenants to humans? What did God promise in this covenant? To whom did He make this promise? How does establishing this covenant relate to earlier promises in 6:18 and 8:22? How was the deliverance of Noah an evidence of God's faithfulness? What shows the commitment of God and our commitment to life?

Verses 8-11: And God spake unto Noah, and to his sons with him, saying, [9]And I, behold, I establish my covenant with you, and with your seed after you; [10]and with every living creature that is with you, of the fowl, of the cattle, and of every beast of the earth with you; from all that go out of the ark, to every beast of the earth. [11]And I will establish my covenant with you; neither shall all flesh be cut off anymore by the waters of a flood; neither shall there anymore be a flood to destroy the earth.

As noted in the "Word Study," the word for **covenant** in the Old Testament always refers to a solemn commitment. In covenants of God and humans, God always takes the initiative. He acts by His sovereign grace to extend His covenant to people. He was under no obligation to make this covenant with Noah and humanity, but He chose to do so. He had told Noah before the flood, "with thee will I establish my covenant" (6:18). Now He said, **Behold, I establish my covenant with you, and with your seed** ("descendants," NIV) **after you.**

Although the Lord was speaking to Noah, He was including in the covenant all people and all living things. Verse 10 spells this out. The covenant with Noah includes all of us of all times. The words **all flesh** and **every living creature** are found over and over in verses 10-17.

Of what does this covenant consist? What was God's promise to Noah and to us? He promised never again **to destroy the earth** by a **flood.** Verse 11 makes this clear and explicit. However, notice that God did not promise that the earth would last forever. Nor did He promise that He would not punish sinners. Neither did He promise that no floods would destroy some people. We know that the last of these happens, and the Bible assures us that unrepentant sinners will face judgment and that this earth will come to an end in God's time and way.

The promise not to destroy the earth by flood was made without conditions on humans. This does not mean that the covenant does not have certain expectations of us in response to God's promise. We noted some of these in verses 1-6. Shortly after departing from the ark and offering a sacrifice to the Lord, Noah heard the Lord promise that part of His promise was this: "While the earth remaineth, seedtime and harvest, and cold and heat, and summer and winter, and day and night shall not cease" (8:22). This was an implication of the promise not to destroy the earth by water. What expectations does this make of humans? These are not spelled out, but one surely is that the Lord expects people to live within the cycles of life as He has ordained them.

How did God show His commitment, and how should we show our commitment, to life?

1. God established His covenant with all living beings. No one was excluded.

2. God promised never again to destroy living things with a global flood. This was a promise of life and an act of grace. But this was a voluntary act of God's grace. Humans have no automatic claim on God because of it.

3. God promised that the seasons and days would be regular and standard. This consistency in nature is necessary for ongoing human life and activities. Our response ought to be to respect and live within the cycles of life ordained by God.

Sign of Remembrance (Gen. 9:12-17)

What is wrong with people demanding signs from God? How should people respond when God gives a sign? Of what was the rainbow a sign? In what sense is the rainbow a reminder to God? How does the covenant with Noah and its sign point toward the larger purpose of God for abundant life and human life? Why do some have a cynical view of life? Why do others have confident hope even when life is at its worst?

Verses 12-17: **And God said, This is the token of the covenant which I make between me and you and every living creature that is with you, for perpetual generations:** [13]**I do set my bow in the cloud, and it shall be for a token of a covenant between me and the earth.** [14]**And it shall come to pass, when I bring a cloud over the earth, that the bow shall be seen in the cloud:** [15]**and I will remember my covenant, which is between me and you and every living creature of all flesh; and the waters shall no more become a flood to destroy all flesh.** [16]**And the bow shall be in the cloud; and I will look upon it, that I may remember the everlasting covenant between God and every living creature of all flesh that is upon the earth.** [17]**And God said unto Noah, This is the token of the covenant, which I have established between me and all flesh that is upon the earth.**

The word translated **token** is usually translated "sign" (NIV). This is the same word as in Isaiah 7:11,14. The word refers to something that points beyond itself to something more significant. The Bible condemns people who demand that God give them signs for them to believe and do the will of God (Matt. 12:38-39). However, the Bible also condemns those who refuse to accept and act on the signs that God gives. God offered to give a sign to Ahaz, which the wicked king piously refused. Then the Lord told him that He was giving him a sign anyway (Isa. 7:11-14).

God gave Noah and all humanity a sign of His covenant after the flood. The Hebrew word *qeset* means a **bow** used with arrows by warriors, but in some passages the word refers to a "rainbow" (NIV). What is the meaning of the sign of the rainbow? It seems to picture God hanging up His war bow as a sign of victory over evil and of peace with humanity. Its placement in the clouds points to the cessation of God's hostilities against mankind. More broadly, therefore, it is a sign of life, hope, and peace.

Verses 14-15 are interesting. We might expect God to emphasize that the rainbow would become a sign to humans, but instead He stressed that it would be a reminder to Him of His promise. Is God subject to lapses of memory? Does He need to be reminded of His promises and of His need to be faithful? The answer to both questions is no. Language from a human point of view is used here of God. God needs no reminder, but we do; therefore, He tells us that even He is reminded of His promise by the rainbow. In this way, we are assured of God's faithfulness to His promise.

Elsewhere in the Bible the rainbow is used as a sign of the greatness and glory of God (Ezek. 1:28; Rev. 4:3). Thus in a sense the rainbow is a sign that the God who saved Noah and his family and made a new start with sinful humanity has an ultimate plan to save sinful humanity from sin and death. Life is not easy. We pass through many storms. Without clouds and storms, there would be no rainbows. Some people become cynical about human life and existence. The "Life Question" for this lesson asks, "How can I have hope about life when so much seems wrong?" Those who know God and the life He gives (a life that the New Testament tells us is abundant and eternal) have confident hope that enables them to affirm God and the life He gives.

Among the most cynical words are these that Shakespeare put into the mouth of Macbeth:

Life's but a walking shadow, a poor player
That struts and frets his hour upon the stage
And then is heard no more: it is a tale
Told by an idiot, full of sound and fury,
Signifying nothing.[1]

Henry Longfellow expressed the opposite view in "A Psalm of Life."

Life is real! Life is earnest!
And the grave is not its goal;
Dust thou art, to dust returnest,
Was not spoken of the soul.[2]

Viktor Frankl endured and survived one of the Nazi concentration camps. In his book *Man's Search for Meaning,* he described how every aspect of existence in the camp was designed to strip human beings of every vestige of human identify, dignity, and hope. Each prisoner was stripped of all possessions. Each became a number, not a name. They were driven and worked like animals until their strength gave out. Then they were herded into gas chambers and exterminated.

Frankl noted how the concentration camp mirrored the paradox of human existence in modern times: "After all, man is that being who has invented the gas chambers of Auschwitz; however, he is also that being who has entered those gas chambers upright, with the Lord's Prayer or the *Shema Yisrael* on his lips."[3]

How did God show His commitment to life and how should we do the same?

1. God gave the rainbow as a lasting sign of His grace toward sinful humanity, thus pointing to the ultimate redemption planned by God. We should be sure that we are among those who know God's abundant and eternal life.

2. The rainbow shines through the clouds of human existence to call us to maintain confident hope in God's promises in the face of life's storms.

❖ *Spiritual Transformations*

In "Search the Scriptures" we have seen how God dealt with Noah and through him with all humanity. God reaffirmed some aspects of His original creation: procreation as the means of continuing the human race, human dominion over animals, and humans made in the image of God. However, animals feared man, who was given permission to eat animals, as long as the blood was not included in what was eaten. Animals, and especially humans, were to be held accountable for shedding human blood. God earlier had promised a covenant with Noah; now He made a covenant with Noah and all living beings. God promised never again to destroy all living beings with a flood. He gave the rainbow in the clouds as a sign of this covenant. It would remind God of His promise and assure humans of God's faithfulness.

The *Life Impact* focuses on forming a biblical view about the value and future of life. In order to build such a view, emphasis has been given to finding in the Focal Passage evidences of God's commitment to life and identifying appropriate human responses. Review these evidences and underline those that seem most significant to you.

Name three evidences of God's commitment to life that impress you. _____

_____

_____

What responses does this lesson call for from you? _____

_____

Prayer of Commitment: Lord, I praise You as the Giver of life—physical, abundant, and eternal. Amen.

[1]Bergen Evans, *Dictionary of Quotations* [New York: Avenel Press, 1968], 391.
[2]Evans, *Dictionary of Quotations*, 392.
[3]Viktor Frankl, *Man's Search for Meaning* [New York: Washington Square Press, 1963], 213-214.

BLESSING ALL NATIONS

Background Passage: Genesis 17:1-27
Focal Passage: Genesis 17:1-8,15-22
Key Verse: Genesis 17:4

❖ *Significance of the Lesson*

• The *Theme* of this lesson is that God's covenant relationship with Abraham included that God would use Abraham to bless all peoples.

• The *Life Question* this lesson seeks to address is, What concern should I have for nations other than my own?

• The *Biblical Truth* is that God promised Abraham that he would be the start of a special nation through which other nations would know of God.

• The *Life Impact* is to help you extend God's blessing by helping all people have an opportunity to know the one, true God.

Attitudes Toward Other Nations

The prevailing secular attitude toward other nations places primary emphasis on our own nation. If some Americans are concerned about other nations, their concern does not include their spiritual needs. As far as missionary work is concerned, secular people neither believe in nor participate in it. They feel that each nation's religion ought to be enough and that missionaries intrude on other nations' cultures.

Those who hold to the biblical worldview are committed to the Great Commission. People are lost without Christ. Therefore, believers are called by God to make Him known to all people. They see the missionary theme running throughout the Bible, with God's promise to Abraham as an early evidence of God's universal concern and His plan to offer His love to all people.

Word Study: *Blessed*

The Hebrew word for **bless** and **blessed** is *barak*. It is found numerous times in the biblical account of Abraham. Genesis 12:2-3 are the key verses. God promised to bless Abram, and He told him to be a blessing. Most importantly, God promised Abraham, "In thee shall all families of the earth be blessed." In our Focal Passage in chapter 17, the word *barak* is used in verses 16 and 20 of Sarah and Ishmael. When Sarah was 90 years old, God promised to bless her with a son and to make her the mother of nations. He also told her that "kings of people" would come from her. God told Abraham that his son Ishmael would be fruitful and multiply exceedingly. He promised that 12 princes would come from him and that Ishmael would become a great nation.

❖ Search the Scriptures

When Abram was 99 years old, God called him to walk before Him and be blameless. God renewed His covenant with Abraham, emphasizing that it was to result in Abraham's becoming the father of many nations. God told Abraham that Sarah would have a son through whom God would continue the covenant.

Covenant Expectations (Gen. 17:1-2)

What were Abraham's ages mentioned in Genesis? What title was used for God? What did God expect of Abram? How does verse 2 relate to earlier messages about the covenant with Abram? What promise did God make in verse 2?

Verses 1-2: And when Abram was ninety years old and nine, the LORD appeared to Abram, and said unto him, I am the Almighty God; walk before me, and be thou perfect. ²And I will make my covenant between me and thee, and will multiply thee exceedingly.

This event happened when Abram was 99 years old. When Abram arrived in Canaan, he was 75 (12:4). He had grown up in Ur, a city in what later became Babylonia. His ancestors worshiped idols, but somehow Abram became a believer in the one true God. His father Terah, along with his family, moved to Haran. God called Abram to go to a land He would show him. God also made the promises of Genesis

12:1-3. Abraham was 86 years old when Ishmael was born (16:16). Between the ages of 75 and 86 several things happened: Abraham and his nephew Lot split up to avoid conflict between their herdsmen. Lot settled in the rich Jordan Valley near Sodom. When enemy kings captured Lot, Abram rescued him. On the way back Abram gave tithes to Melchizedek. God made a covenant with Abram. Sarai gave her servant Hagar to Abram to have a child. The Bible tells us nothing about the silent years between ages 86 and 99.

God had promised Abram many descendants, but Abram was growing older and his wife also was growing older. With each passing year the possibility of their having a child of their own seemed to grow less likely. How do you suppose Abram felt about God and His promise during those silent years? Most of us would have been tempted to believe that God had forgotten us. We need to remember that the eternal God does not operate on our time schedules.

God revealed Himself to Abram as **the Almighty God.** In Hebrew this is *El Shaddai.* Most modern translations see it as a title stressing the power of God. This surely fits the context here. From a human point of view, it was impossible for this elderly couple to have a child of their own. From the divine point of view, all things are possible with God. God is able to fulfill His promises in His own time and way.

Abram's acceptance by God was based on God's grace and Abram's faith (15:6). In Genesis 17:1 there is an emphasis on the kind of life lived by a person of true faith. God saves us on the basis of His grace through our faith, but He has expectations of His saved people. Two expectations are mentioned in verse 1. **Walk before me** is the moral result of walking with the Lord. It means to live in such a way in the sight of God that our lives are pleasing to Him. **Be thou perfect** reminds us of the words of Jesus, "Be ye therefore perfect, even as your Father which is in heaven is perfect" (Matt. 5:48). These verses trouble us because we know that no one but Jesus ever lived a sinlessly perfect life. But look at it from the perspective of the Heavenly Father. Many of us are parents. Which of us would say to our children, "Be 90 percent honest or good"? No, we tell them to be 100 percent honest and good. When they fall short, we forgive them and help them do better, but we do not lower our expectations for them to be the best they can be.

Genesis 15 records the first time that God made His covenant with Abram. He repeated and amplified on earlier promises, and Abram believed Him. In those days, covenants were often made by cutting animals in half as a sign of the covenant. The repeated mention of a **covenant** in chapter 17 is not a different covenant but a renewal of the earlier one. In the covenant God promised to **multiply** Abram **exceedingly.**

What lasting truths are found in these verses?

1. God does not operate on our time schedules. From our point of view, He seems to be delaying; however, He will keep His promises in His own time and in His own way.

2. God Almighty has the power to do what seems impossible by human standards.

3. God expects His people to walk with Him in faith and to walk before Him in a way pleasing to Him.

4. God renews His covenants with His people from time to time.

Many Nations and One God (Gen. 17:3-8)

In what sense was Abram a father of many nations? Why did God change Abram's name? Why did God call this an everlasting covenant? Who was the seed of Abraham? What are the missionary implications of faith in one true God?

Verses 3-5: **And Abram fell on his face: and God talked with him, saying, [4]As for me, behold, my covenant is with thee, and thou shalt be a father of many nations. [5]Neither shall thy name anymore be called Abram, but thy name shall be Abraham; for a father of many nations have I made thee.**

Abram's reverence for God is seen in the fact that when God spoke to him, **Abram fell on his face.** As he bowed reverently, **God talked with him.** God reassured him, **My covenant is with thee.** Then God told Abram that he would **be a father of many nations.** Paul quoted this title in Romans 4:17-18. The apostle explained that those who have a faith like Abraham's faith are his children. They are heirs of the promises to Abraham. This was shocking to many of Paul's fellow Jews because many of them insisted that only the children of Abraham were his physical descendants. This is a key point in seeing the missionary theme in the life of Abraham. It makes the same basic point as Genesis 12:3. It is repeated at other crucial times in his life. For example, in connection with the prayer for Sodom, God said, "Abraham shall surely become a great and mighty nation, and all the nations of the earth shall be blessed in him" (18:18). After Abraham passed the test on Mount Moriah by showing his willingness to sacrifice his beloved son Isaac, God's angel told him, "In thy seed shall all the nations of the earth be blessed; because thou hast obeyed my voice" (22:18). Essentially the same promise was repeated when God passed along the covenant to Isaac (26:4) and to Jacob (28:14).

Because of this significant renewal of the covenant, Genesis 17:5 tells us that God changed the name of **Abram** to **Abraham.** Names were more significant in Bible times than they are today. **Abram** means "exalted father." **Abraham** means "father of many." His new name fitted his new title as **father of many nations.**

God had made a new start with Noah and his sons after the flood, but humanity continued in its sinful ways. God made another new start with Abraham. It was a different kind of start than the one with Noah. God selected one man and his descendants as the ones through whom to bring redemption to the whole world. Unfortunately, some of Abraham's descendants failed to see the purposes for which God chose them—to be a missionary people and a blessing to all peoples.

Verses 6-8: **And I will make thee exceeding fruitful, and I will make nations of thee, and kings shall come out of thee. [7]And I will establish my covenant between me and thee and thy seed after thee in their generations for an everlasting covenant, to be a God unto thee, and to thy seed after thee. [8]And I will give unto thee, and to thy seed after thee, the land wherein thou art a stranger, all the land of Canaan, for an everlasting possession; and I will be their God.**

God promised Abraham, **I will make nations of thee, and kings shall come out of thee.** The genealogy of Jesus in Matthew 1:1-17 shows how David and all of David's royal line were descendants of Abraham. The ultimate King of this line was and is Jesus Christ.

The word **seed** is prominent in the covenant with Abraham. The first seed of Abraham in the line of promise was Isaac, whose birth is told in Genesis 21. In a sense, all of Abraham's descendants were his seed. However, the New Testament says that the ultimate seed of Abraham was Jesus Christ (Gal. 3:16-17). Through Christ the promises of God to Abraham were fulfilled. Through Jesus Christ the Savior of the world God sends forth the message of His love to all people. We who have faith in Jesus are children of God and, in a sense, children of Abraham because we come to God by Abraham's kind of faith and seek to fulfill God's purpose of making the good news known to all people.

God called the covenant with Abraham **an everlasting covenant.** This was no temporary covenant designed to give way to another covenant later. This places the Abrahamic covenant in a higher category than the covenant of law at Mount Sinai. The Abrahamic covenant was designed to lead people to faith. The new covenant with Jesus Christ is the fulfillment and continuation of the covenant of faith with Abraham. If we believe that the one God has sent His Son to be the one Savior of all people, we cannot withhold the good news of Jesus Christ from anyone.

What lasting truths are in these verses?

1. God's purpose always has been to offer salvation to all people of all nations.

2. God chose Abraham to make a new start toward achieving His purpose.

3. Jesus Christ is the seed of Abraham who fulfilled the covenant with Abraham.

4. God called Abraham to be the father of many nations. Those who have a faith like Abraham's are children of God as well as children of Abraham.

5. Faith in one God calls on believers in the one God to make Him known to all people.

God-Sized Promise (Gen. 17:15-19)

What was Sarah's part in the fulfillment of God's covenant with Abraham? Why did Abraham laugh? Later, why did Sarah laugh? What question did Abraham ask God? Why did Abraham ask that Ishmael might live? What instructions and promises did God make about the son to be born to Abraham and Sarah?

Verses 15-19: And God said unto Abraham, As for Sarai thy wife, thou shalt not call her name Sarai, but Sarah shall her name be. ¹⁶And I will bless her, and give thee a son also of her: yea, I will bless her, and she shall be a mother of nations; kings of people shall be of her. ¹⁷Then Abraham fell upon his face, and laughed, and said in his heart, Shall a child be born unto him that is an hundred years old? and shall Sarah, that is ninety years old, bear? ¹⁸And Abraham said unto God, O that Ishmael might live before thee! ¹⁹And God said, Sarah thy wife shall bear thee a son indeed; and thou shalt call his name Isaac: and I will establish my covenant with him for an everlasting covenant, and with his seed after him.

We are not told why God changed the name of **Sarai** to **Sarah.** One reason was to match the name change of her husband, for she too played a crucial role in the ongoing of God's plan. She became not only the mother of Isaac but also **a mother of nations.** God told Abraham, **I will bless her.** Sarah thus was crucial in fulfilling God's plan to make of Abraham a great nation that would bless all nations.

When Abraham realized that God was telling him that he and Sarah were to have a son in their old age, Abraham responded in three ways that at first sight seem to be something other than the faith he showed at other times. First, **Abraham fell upon his face, and laughed.** We wonder in what sense he **laughed.** Assuming the best, he may have laughed with wonder and joy, not with doubt and skepticism. God did not rebuke Abraham for laughing. Yet in 18:12, when Sarah overheard God tell Abraham that within a year she would bear a son, she laughed. God asked Abraham, "Why did Sarah laugh?" (NIV). Sarah quickly "lied and said, 'I did not laugh.' But he said, 'Yes, you did laugh'" (v. 15, NIV). Why did God call Sarah's hand but not Abraham's? Perhaps the situation was like that involving conversations of Gabriel with Zachariah and with Mary. Each of them asked basically the same question. Zachariah, however, was punished for unbelief and Mary was honored for her faith (Luke 1:18-20,34-35). Perhaps God, who sees our hearts, saw faith in Abraham's laughter and doubt in Sarah's. At any rate, God told them to name their son **Isaac,** which means "he who laughs." When Isaac was born, Sarah said, "God hath made me to laugh, so that all that hear will laugh with me" (21:6). Whatever the motivation for her laughter in chapter 18, in chapter 21 she laughed in joy and wonder.

Abraham's second response was to ask God a straight question: "Will a son be born to a man a hundred years old? Will Sarah bear a child at the age of ninety?" (17:17, NIV). The honest and candid question is typical of the questions of many Old Testament people of faith. God seems to have taken Abraham's question as an expression of seeking faith and earnest prayer.

Abraham's third response was to say, **O that Ishmael might live before thee!** Genesis 16 tells the story of Ishmael. His birth resulted from the efforts of Sarah and Abraham to provide a child for Abraham by human means. According to the custom of that day, a barren wife could give her servant to her husband and the child would be considered the child of the man and his wife. Sarah sent Hagar to Abraham, and the result was the birth of Ishmael. After Ishmael was born, Sarah became vindictive and had Abraham send Hagar away, along with Ishmael, but the Lord cared for them. Abraham, feeling that he and Sarah were too old to have a son, seems to have asked the Lord to reconsider using Ishmael as the promised heir. At the very least, Abraham was asking that the Lord watch over Ishmael.

One translation of the transition word from verse 18 to verse 19 is "Yes, but" (NIV). In other words, God was reassuring Abraham that He would care for Ishmael but that His plan was to continue the line of promise through the child of promise. God made several points about what Abraham and Sarah were to do. First, God repeated His promise that **Sarah** would **bear** this child. God told them the child's **name** was to be **Isaac.** God made clear the fact that the **everlasting covenant** with Abraham was to continue through Isaac.

The promise of a son to people their ages was a "God-sized promise." Only God could bring such a miracle. But as the Lord asked Sarah when she laughed, "Is anything too hard for the LORD?" (18:14).

What lasting truths are in these verses?

1. Sarah was to become the mother of many nations.

2. When God makes a promise, the laughter of joy and wonder is more appropriate than laughter of doubt and cynicism.

3. God accepts honest questions addressed to Him as prayers. He does not always give what to us would seem to be a clear, rational answer, but He does respond in His own way.

4. Attempts to achieve by human methods what only God can do are doomed to failure.

5. God is able to do all that is needed to fulfill His promises.

Blessing Other Nations (Gen. 17:20-22)

What promises did God make about Ishmael? How do the words about Ishmael imply a concern for more that the descendants of Isaac? How did God promise to continue the covenant with Abraham?

Verses 20-22: And as for Ishmael, I have heard thee: Behold, I have blessed him, and will make him fruitful, and will multiply him exceedingly; twelve princes shall he beget, and I will make him a great nation. ²¹But my covenant will I establish with Isaac, which Sarah shall bear unto thee at this set time in the next year. ²²And he left off talking with him, and God went up from Abraham.

Concerning Ishmael, God assured Abraham that He had **heard** Abraham's concerned prayer on Ishmael's behalf. God promised several things about Abraham's other son. God said, **I have blessed him.** He promised, **I . . . will make him fruitful, and will multiply him exceedingly.** Like Israel, Ishmael would have **twelve princes.** God promised to **make him a great nation.** This shows that God has always been concerned about the descendants of Ishmael. Many of them today are followers of Mohammed. God is concerned for them, as well as for the descendants of Isaac and Jacob. Some of the most challenging mission fields today are among the descendants of Ishmael. Many are militant Moslems, but some have become Christians.

Although Ishmael was on God's heart, His plan was to be continued through Isaac—**my covenant will I establish with Isaac.** When we ask why God chose Isaac instead of Ishmael, we get into divine sovereignty. God has the right to make His own choices. Besides, Isaac was born as a child of faith through a miracle of God, whereas Ishmael was born in an attempt to achieve divine purposes by human means.

What lasting truth is in these verses? God cared about Ishmael, and He cares about his descendants, but He chose to fulfill His promise through Isaac, the child of promise.

Ernest Gordon was a British prisoner of war of the Japanese during World War II. He was among prisoners who labored under terrible conditions in the jungles of Thailand. Occasionally, the prisoners met Thai people of various groups. Most of these people treated the prisoners badly. However, one village went all out to help the disease-ridden, starving prisoners. Gordon discovered that the people of that village were Christians, people who had been led to Christ by a Christian woman missionary. The Japanese tried to capture this missionary but they were unsuccessful.

The Christian actions of these Thai believers played a part in the discovery of true Christianity among many of the British prisoners. They saw the practical results of those who have sought to fulfill God's promise to Abraham to send One through whom all nations would be blessed. Christian missionary work is the way to fulfill God's purpose to take the good news to all people.[1]

❖ *Spiritual Transformations*

When Abram was 99 years old, the Lord appeared to him and told him to walk before Him and be blameless. God confirmed the covenant with Abram by changing his name to Abraham, for he was to be a father of many nations. God promised Abraham that Sarah would be the mother of nations. Laughing, Abraham asked how a man of 100 and a woman of 90 could have a child. Abraham asked that Ishmael might live before God. God promised blessings on Ishmael but reaffirmed that the son of promise would be born to Sarah and would be named Isaac.

By their faith in God, all believers today become spiritual children of Abraham. That is, all believers are Abraham's seed or Abraham's descendants by faith. The "Life Impact" picks up on God's promise to bless all nations through Abraham and his seed—to help you extend God's blessing by helping all people have an opportunity to know the one true God. This missionary theme is foundational for later biblical teaching on missions. The Bible clearly calls all believers to be Great Commission Christians.

What are some of the more explicit Bible passages about missions?

_____

What basis do you have for considering yourself to be a Great Commission Christian? _____

_____

Prayer of Commitment: Lord, help me to be a Great Commission Christian. Amen.

[1]Ernest Gordon, *Through the Valley of the Kwai* [New York: Harper & Row, Publishers, 1962], 94.

CREATING A DISTINCTIVE PEOPLE

Background Passage: Exodus 19–20
Focal Passage: Exodus 19:5-6; 20:1-4,7-10a,12-17
Key Verses: Exodus 19:5-6a

❖ *Significance of the Lesson*

• The *Theme* of this lesson is that God's covenant relationship with Moses included God's giving His people rules for living.
• The *Life Question* this lesson seeks to address is, What kind of lifestyle does God want me to have?
• The *Biblical Truth* is that in the Ten Commandments, God revealed basic principles that shape the lifestyles of His people to reflect His distinctive character.
• The *Life Impact* is to help you live in full obedience to God's law.

Moral Standards

The secular worldview denies that absolute moral standards should govern human conduct. In other words, right and wrong are relative. Each person decides in each situation what is right and what is wrong. Those who do give lip service to standards based on the Ten Commandments often rationalize disobedience when the payoff is enough.

According to the biblical worldview, God revealed abiding moral standards based on His own character. God expects people to live by these standards and warned against violating them.

Word Study: *peculiar treasure*

These two English words translate one Hebrew word. Page Kelley stated about this word: "It is a relatively rare word, being used only eight times in the entire Old Testament. Of these uses, two refer to the private treasure of a king (1 Chron. 29:3; Eccl. 2:8), and six refer symbolically to Israel as God's special treasure or possession (Ex. 19:5; Deut. 7:6; 14:2; 26:18; Ps. 135:4; Mal. 3:17). This term passed over into the New Testament by way of the Septuagint [the Greek transla-tion of the Old Testament] and came to be used to represent the Christian's unique relationship to God through Christ (Eph. 1:14; 2 Thess. 2:14; Titus 2:14; 1 Pet. 2:9)."[1]

❖ Search the Scriptures

Having delivered Israel from Egypt, the Lord led the Israelites to Mount Sinai where He offered a covenant to the people. He said that if they kept the covenant, they would be His special possession among all people, a kingdom of priests, and a holy nation. God gave the Israelites the Ten Commandments. The first two Commandments call for a dis-tinctive relationship with God. The next two focus on distinctive reverence for God, and the last six deal with distinctive treatment of other people.

Call to Be Distinctive (Ex. 19:5-6)

*What was the setting for these words? What is the significance of the word **if**? What did God expect of His people? In what three ways did He describe His people? What evidence is there that God's ultimate plan was to include all people?*

19:5-6: Now therefore, if ye will obey my voice indeed, and keep my covenant, then ye shall be a peculiar treasure unto me above all people: for all the earth is mine: ⁶And ye shall be unto me a king-dom of priests, and an holy nation. These are the words which thou shalt speak unto the children of Israel.

Therefore points back to verse 4, which points back to everything earlier in the Book of Exodus. God's deliverance of His people from Egyp-tian slavery was the basis on which He offered them this **covenant.**

If shows that the covenant was not being forced on them. They could choose or reject it. It also shows that the fulfillment of God's promises to them depended on their own meeting of God's expectations for them.

Obey in Hebrew is the same word as "hear." Literally, it reads, "if listening you will listen." In the eyes of the Lord, hearing His Word always ought to lead us to obey Him. **Keep my covenant** says the same thing with different words. As with all the covenants in which God is a party, God initiated the covenant at Mount Sinai. He offered Himself to Israel as their God, based on His actions on their behalf. They were expected to be obedient.

God used three ways to describe the covenant relationship. First, they would be His **peculiar treasure.** The meaning of the English word *peculiar* has changed since 1611 when the *King James Version* was translated. The meaning here is not "strange" but "special." (See the "Word Study.") An ancient king owned many valuable things, but he might have a special treasure of greatest value to him. Even so, God owns all things and all people. Yet here He began a new phase in His redemptive work by choosing the descendants of Israel to be His in a special way.

Israel was chosen to be God's instrument to reach out to all people. This truth is also evident in the second title for the Israelites. They were to be **a kingdom of priests.** This phrase can mean that each of them was to serve as a priest. "You will be my holy nation and serve me as priests" (CEV). More likely, however, the idea is that they were to be a "priestly kingdom" (NRSV). A priest has access to God, which is used to bring others close to God. Israel was to be a missionary people through whom the Lord would work to influence other people to come to God.

The third title for Israel is **an holy nation.** The word **holy** basically means "to be set apart." At times the word has no moral connotation, but when used of God and His people, the word came to have a strong moral meaning. "At first, no doubt 'holy' merely meant 'dedicated' to God without any particular moral connotations. Such 'holiness' was contagious (Ex. 19:12) and might be dangerous, if not fatal. Then, because of the revealed nature of YHWH, such 'holiness,' as descriptive of God, took on a strong moral meaning. Ultimately God's holiness became a compelling moral demand on his people (see Lv. 20:7)."[2]

The faith of Israel has been called ethical monotheism. The Israelites believed in one God, in contrast to the many gods of other nations. And this one God is holy and He expects His people to be holy. They are to reflect the character of God. The people of Israel were called to a distinctive faith and way of living. Throughout most of the Old Testament, they compromised their distinctives. Finally they were punished for it by being sent into exile. After the exile, they seem to have learned the need to be distinctive, but many of them failed to see that the purpose of being God's holy people was to bear witness to all nations of the holy Lord.

What are the lasting truths of these verses?

1. God offers covenants to people.
2. God chooses some to be His people.
3. Those God chooses are called to be holy.
4. God's people are to be a missions people.

Distinctive Relationship with God (Ex. 20:1-4)

Why are the Ten Commandments foundational to human life? Why is the First Commandment foundational for the Ten Commandments? How do various groups divide the Ten Commandments? What is the distinctive of the First Commandment? How does the Second Commandment differ from the First? In what ways are these commandments broken today?

20:1-2: And God spake all these words, saying, [2]I am the Lord thy God, which have brought thee out of the land of Egypt, out of the house of bondage.

Verse 1 emphasizes the source of these Commandments: **God spake all these words.** "The commandments are God's nature expressed in terms of moral imperatives."[3]

The Jews consider verse 2 to be the First Commandment. Verses 3-6 then are called the Second Commandment. Roman Catholics and Lutherans combine verses 3-6 as the First Commandment and divide verse 17 into two commandments. Most Protestants see verse 2 as a preamble, verse 3 as the First, and verses 4-6 as the Second Commandment.

Just as Exodus 19:4 tied the making of the covenant to the deliverance from Egypt, so does 20:2 tie the Ten Commandments to the same event. **I am the Lord thy God** identifies the One who spoke these Commandments. This is the One who led the exodus from Egyptian bondage—**which have brought thee out of the land of Egypt, out of the house of bondage.** The Old Testament never refers to this as an escape engineered by humans but as a deliverance that only God could bring to pass. When Moses went to Pharaoh and told him that the Lord called on him to let the Lord's people go, Pharaoh haughtily asked, "Who is the Lord, that I should obey his voice to let Israel go?" (5:2). The Lord's answer, "I am the Lord," was repeated throughout the chapters that followed (6:2,6,7,8,29; 7:5; 10:2).

20:3: Thou shalt have no other gods before me.

The Ten Commandments are foundational for human life. Many people today believe that we have outgrown the need for these ancient rules for living. They especially feel that this is true of the first four Commandments about our relationship with God. They feel that they can keep the moral and social commandments without needing God. Nothing could be further from the truth. Only God can enable us to keep the Commandments.

The First Commandment recognizes that many people worshiped other gods. It does not recognize the reality of these gods, but it recognizes that many people worship these nonexistent gods as if they are real.

The Commandment shows the need for exclusive worship of the one God. If there were many gods, people's devotion would need to be spread out among many. This Commandment calls for no other gods to be placed **before** the one true God. Whatever comes first in our lives is our god.

***20:4:* Thou shalt not make unto thee any graven image, or any likeness of anything that is in heaven above, or that is in the earth beneath, or that is in the water under the earth.**

The Second Commandment, which extends through verse 6, seems at first glance merely to repeat the First; however, on closer inspection, we can see a difference. The First forbids worshiping other gods; the Second forbids trying to worship God by making images to represent Him. When you study the archaeological remains of ancient civilizations, most of those civilizations had statues and images to represent their gods. The Hebrews had no such images of their God.

The danger of making images of God is that no image that we make can adequately depict the majesty of the eternal God. Images always give a limited picture of the Lord. This is true not only of images of stone, wood, and metal but also of our mental images of God. We form our own pictures of God, and none of them is big enough to depict the Lord of heaven and earth.

What are the lasting lessons from these verses?

1. God is the source of the Ten Commandments.

2. These Commandments are foundational for human society.

3. Only as God is Lord of our lives can we hope to keep the moral and social Commandments.

4. Not only are we to have no other gods, but we also are not to form images of God.

Distinctive Reverence for God (Ex. 20:7-10a)

*What is the meaning of **in vain**? Why are names important in the Bible? In what ways is the Third Commandment broken? What does **sabbath** mean? How does the Sabbath speak to both work and rest? What was the attitude of Jesus toward the Sabbath? Why do Christians meet to worship on Sunday instead of Saturday?*

20:7: Thou shalt not take the name of the LORD thy God in vain; for the LORD will not hold him guiltless that taketh his name in vain.

Verse 7 sets forth the Third Commandment. It is designed to protect God's **name.** In ancient times, names were more significant than today. A name represented the person named. **The name of the LORD** thus represents **God.** The Hebrew word for **in vain** means "emptily," "falsely," "deceitfully." Thus God's name is taken in vain when it is used in any of these ways. To put it another way, the name of God ought to be honored, blessed, praised, glorified, invoked, celebrated, and shared. It ought not to be used profanely, irreverently, or emptily. "Do not misuse my name" (CEV).

People use God's name profanely when they blaspheme the name of God. They curse God and say many evil things about Him. God said that He will hold people accountable for how they use His name. People use God's name irreverently when they swear or exclaim words that include the name of God. In recent years on television this has become common, even among so-called decent people. They use God's name whenever they are excited.

Even religious people take God's name in vain when we use His name in an empty way. Perfunctory prayers and songs of praise may break this commandment. Jesus condemned those who drew near to God with their lips but their hearts were far from Him (Matt. 15:8). "Lip service" is a deadly expression of violating this Commandment. When we use God's name without truly worshiping Him, we commit this sin. Even more serious is the use of God's name in worship when the so-called worshiper is living in sin.

20:8-10a: Remember the sabbath day, to keep it holy. ⁹Six days shalt thou labor, and do all thy work: ¹⁰ᵃbut the seventh day is the sabbath of the LORD thy God.

The Fourth Commandment is the first of the Ten to be stated positively. **Remember** is an important Old Testament word. It means more than recalling something; it involves recalling and acting on what is remembered. The meaning of **sabbath** is "rest" or "cessation." Thus on **the seventh day** the people of Israel were called to rest. We must not forget, however, that the Fourth Commandment calls for both **work** and rest. Just as God worked for **six days** and rested on **the seventh,** so are His people to do the same.

The day was to be kept **holy,** that is, set apart for the Lord. The setting aside of one day in seven signifies that every day belongs to the Lord.

From the social and economic perspective, this Commandment was designed to free working people from the tyranny of ceaseless toil. Notice in verse 10 that each was to apply it not only to himself but also to his family and all who worked for him. Without this Commandment, workers could be forced to toil every day.

The need for one day out of seven to be set apart for rest and renewal is built into the cycle of human life. Those who disregard it do so at their peril. Too many of us are workaholics, who work all the time. As the Sabbath developed, it became not only a day of rest but also a day for worshiping and for studying the Scriptures (see Luke 4:16-39; Acts 13:14). Our Lord Jesus honored the Sabbath Day, but He condemned those who had defeated its purpose with their human traditions. As Christians, we keep the first day of the week— Sunday—as our time for rest and spiritual renewal because Jesus was raised from the dead on the first day of the week (Luke 24:1; Acts 20:7; 1 Cor. 16:2).

What lasting lessons are in these verses?

1. We are to honor God's name, not to profane it.

2. We are to balance work and rest according the cycles of life set forth by God.

Distinctive Treatment of Other People (Ex. 20:12-17)

What human rights are the last six Commandments designed to protect? In what ways is each of these Commandments broken? How could each Commandment be stated positively?

20:12: **Honor thy father and thy mother: that thy days may be long upon the land which the LORD thy God giveth thee.**

The Fifth Commandment is the first of six that focus on human relations. It is designed to protect the basic institution of society— the family. Two Commandments provide the basis for this foundational human institution. The Fifth Commandment focuses on parents and children; the Seventh focuses on marriage.

The Bible generally applies the content of the Fifth Commandment to grown children and their need to respect and care for their aging parents (Mark 7:1-13; 1 Tim. 5:4). But Paul also applied it to children's need to obey their parents (Eph. 6:1-3). Younger children should obey and respect their parents; all children of all ages should respect them. This respect includes caring for the parents in their old age.

The many dysfunctional families in today's society show the need for reemphasizing this basic expectation of the Lord. Many parents and their children are alienated from each other. When a parent dies under such conditions, their offspring experience great burdens of grief.

20:13: **Thou shalt not kill.**

This is the first of three Commandments consisting of six consonants in Hebrew. **Kill** translates a word that refers to murder rather than to killing in general. Many translations have the word "murder" (NIV, NKJV, NASB, NRSV, NEB, REB, CEV). The word does not apply to unintentional accidents, although the result in each is the loss of a precious human life. The Commandment is directed against premeditated murder. Such murder can be committed by the person himself or by someone acting on behalf of the one who wants a person murdered. **Thou** is the second person singular; thus, it is addressed to each person.

The Sixth Commandment is designed to protect and preserve human life. Once a life is taken, it cannot be retrieved. In Shakespeare's tragedy *Othello,* an evil man convinced Othello that his wife Desdemona had been unfaithful. Filled with angry jealousy, Othello went to murder his wife. As he made his way toward her room, he commented on the candle in his hand. He said that if he blew out the candle, he could relight it; however, he realized that if he murdered Desdemona, he could not recall her to life. After murdering her, he was filled with guilt and remorse, so much so that he took his own life.[4]

20:14: **Thou shalt not commit adultery.**

The Seventh Commandment is designed to protect the basic foundation of the family, the relationship of husband and wife. **Adultery** refers to an act of unfaithfulness between two persons at least one of whom is married to someone else. This act of sexual immorality undermines the fabric of trust that holds a marriage together. The Bible also condemns any sexual act that perverts God's good purpose for sex. God intended that sexual relations be the means by which a man and a woman become one flesh and thus make a lifetime commitment to each other in responsible love.

Our culture is a sexual wilderness in which all kinds of sexual sins are promoted, practiced, and permitted. Jesus warned that lust is sinful and often leads to acts of sexual sin (Matt. 5:27-28). Our society feeds the lusts of people in too many ways to mention them all. Out of this come the sins of adultery, fornication, homosexuality, lesbianism, and perversions of all kinds. Using sex to do something other than express the one-flesh union of marriage is like using a scalpel designed for surgery to whittle a piece of wood.

20:15: Thou shalt not steal.

How many words for stealing or the one who steals can you name? Some of these are thief, burglar, con man, pickpocket, extortion, rob, embezzle, kidnap, filch, mug, hold up, rip off, car jack, and on and on. The large and varied list shows how much the Eighth Commandment is broken. The variety of words also shows that this Commandment is broken not only by thieves such as those of Luke 10:30 but also by those who cheat customers, as in Amos 8:5-6, and by those who withhold wages, as in James 5:1-6.

This Commandment is designed to protect one's right to own property and have the use of it. Owning property gives a person freedom from being controlled by the state or by someone else. It also gives one opportunities to help others and to honor God. If we have nothing of our own, we have nothing to give. When someone steals what is ours, the thief takes our ability to meet the needs of our own family and our ability to help others.

20:16: Thou shalt not bear false witness against thy neighbor.

The Ninth Commandment is designed to protect reputation. Violations of this Commandment destroy the reputations of others and can destroy their very lives. The most obvious way the Ninth Commandment is broken is through false testimony in a court of law. However, it also is broken by slander, gossip, and lying.

Many people have had their reputations ruined by gossip. Proverbs 6:16-19 warns of seven things the Lord hates: three of these are "a lying tongue," "a false witness that speaketh lies," and "he that soweth discord among brethren."

20:17: Thou shalt not covet thy neighbor's house, thou shalt not covet thy neighbor's wife, nor his manservant, nor his maidservant, nor his ox, nor his ass, nor anything that is thy neighbor's.

To **covet** is to want something that someone else has. It combines greed and envy. Jesus warned that covetous people miss what life is all about. They equate having possessions with having the good life (Luke 12:13-21). The Tenth Commandment does not forbid a specific act; instead, it condemns an attitude that leads to many of the sins condemned in previous Commandments. Ahab coveted the vineyard of Naboth. After Naboth refused to sell it, Jezebel plotted to get the vineyard. She involved the city officials in hiring false witnesses against

Naboth, breaking the Ninth Commandment. This led to the death of Naboth and his family, breaking the Sixth Commandment. Ahab confiscated the vineyard, breaking the Eighth Commandment. All of this was done in the name of God and the king, breaking the First and Third Commandments.

❖ *Spiritual Transformations*

God offered to Israel a covenant to be His special people. Then He gave them the Ten Commandments to show what obedience to Him means.

Elton Trueblood offered these Commandments in poetic form.

Above all else love God alone;
Bow down to neither wood nor stone.
God's name refuse to take in vain;
The Sabbath rest with care maintain.
Respect your parents all your days;
Hold sacred human life always.
Be loyal to your chosen mate;
Steal nothing, neither small nor great.
Report, with truth, your neighbor's deed;
And rid your mind of selfish greed.[5]

Which of these Commandments is hardest for you to obey? Why?

_____

*What specific steps can you take to be more obedient?*_____

_____

Prayer of Commitment: Almighty God our Father, help me obey all Your Commandments. Amen.

[1]Page H. Kelley, *Exodus: Called for Redemptive Mission* [Nashville: Convention Press, 1977], 95.

[2]R. Alan Cole, *Exodus,* in the Tyndale Old Testament Commentaries [Downers Grove: InterVarsity Press, 1973], 145.

[3]Cole, *Exodus,* 152.

[4]William Shakespeare, *Othello,* Act V, Scene II, lines 7-15.

[5]Elton Trueblood, "The Ten Commandments in Verse," in *Foundations for Reconstruction,* revised edition [New York: Harper & Brothers Publishers, 1961], 11.

PROMISING A RIGHTEOUS RULER

Background Passage: 2 Samuel 7:1-29; Psalm 89:1-52; Isaiah 9:2-7
Focal Passage: 2 Samuel 7:8-16; Psalm 89:1-4; Isaiah 9:6-7
Key Verses: Psalm 89:3-4

❖ *Significance of the Lesson*

• The *Theme* of this lesson is that God's covenant relationship with David included God's promise that David's kingdom would be established forever.

• The *Life Question* this lesson seeks to address is, What does God's promise of an unending kingdom have to do with me?

• The *Biblical Truth* is that God's promise to David of an unending kingdom ultimately pointed to the coming of the Messiah-King to establish God's rule forever.

• The *Life Impact* is to help you live under the authority of God's righteous Ruler.

Attitudes Toward Divine Promises

The prevailing secular mindset does not accept as real the existence of the God of the Bible, much less that this God's purposes and actions have directed the course of history. Thus biblical promises and prophecies are seen as no more than human stories and fables that have little to do with people's lives today. This widespread view causes many people to question the relevance of a divine promise made to a regional monarch who lived 3,000 years ago.

In the biblical worldview, God is real and personal and is the Lord of human history. As such, God made a covenant with David that He would affirm his family line as His chosen rulers forever. God's promise ultimately was fulfilled in the coming of Jesus Christ, the Messiah-King.

Word Study: *Throne*

The Hebrew word *kisse'* can refer to any kind of seat or chair (2 Kings 4:10), but it usually refers to a seat of honor (Isa. 22:23). Mostly it is used for a royal throne (for example, Esth. 5:1). At times it refers to an actual throne on which a king sat. Solomon's throne is described in 1 Kings 10:18-19. Often the word was used figuratively to describe a king's authority to reign. The Old Testament often refers to the throne of God, signifying God as the eternal King. After the covenant with David, many references are made to those who reigned on the throne of David.

❖ *Search the Scriptures*

When David wanted to build God a house, God refused; however, God promised to build a house for David. The house God promised to build for David was a dynasty of David's descendants. God promised that the reign of the house of David would be forever. Pious Israelites affirmed this promise as the basis for their hope in the faithfulness of God. Isaiah foresaw that this promise would be fulfilled in one future King, who would be more than just an earthly king.

A Promise to Count On (2 Sam. 7:8-16)

*At what stage in David's life did God make this promise to David? In what two ways is the word **house** used in this passage? What promise did God make concerning David's immediate descendant? What promise did God make about the security of David's line on the throne? What promise did God make about the enduring quality of David's line?*

2 Samuel 7:8-11: Now therefore so shalt thou say unto my servant David, Thus saith the LORD of hosts, I took thee from the sheepcote, from following the sheep, to be ruler over my people, over Israel: ⁹and I was with thee whithersoever thou wentest, and have cut off all thine enemies out of thy sight, and have made thee a great name, like unto the name of the great men that are in the earth. ¹⁰Moreover I will appoint a place for my people Israel, and will plant them, that they may dwell in a place of their own, and move no more; neither shall the children of wickedness afflict them anymore, as beforetime, ¹¹and as since the time that I commanded judges to

be over my people Israel, and have caused thee to rest from all thine enemies. Also the LORD telleth thee that he will make thee an house.

David was one of the key people of the Old Testament. The account of his life is found in 1 Samuel 16:1–1 Kings 2:11. David's life falls into three parts: (1) His life before he became king; (2) from the time he became king until his great sin; and (3) from his great sin until his death. The biblical account of the promise of God's covenant came within the second period of his life. David was at the pinnacle of his success. He had become king not only over his own tribe of Judah but also over all of Israel. He had captured Jerusalem and made it his capital. He had built a palace and had moved the ark of the covenant to Jerusalem.

After God had given David victory over his enemies and a well-deserved rest from fighting, David told Nathan the prophet that he was bothered by the fact that he lived in a house of cedar but the ark of the covenant still was housed only in a tent (7:1-2). Nathan, without consulting the Lord, told David to proceed to build a house or temple for the Lord (v. 3). The Lord, however, spoke to Nathan and asked him when He, the Lord, had ever asked that a temple be build for Him. Nathan was given a message to deliver to David. This is the point at which verse 8 begins—**Now therefore so shalt thou say unto my servant David.**

My servant carries several messages. For one thing, it reminded David that in spite of his high status as king, he was still a servant of God. Yet the term **servant** was a term of honor for those who served the Lord. This "is an honoured title, but at the same time a reminder to David that, though he is king, and surrounded by those who serve him, he too has his servant role in relation to his God."[1]

God reminded David that everything good in his life had happened because God had caused it to happen. God specifically reminded David that he had been only a shepherd until God **took** him **from the sheepcote** ("pasture," NIV, NASB, NRSV; "sheepfold," NKJV). The biblical account of David's anointing by the prophet Samuel emphasizes how Samuel and David's family would have chosen differently, for although humans look on the outward appearance, God sees the heart (1 Sam. 16:7). God had taken a shepherd boy and made him **ruler over** God's **people, over Israel.**

Each of us can look back over our lives and see how God has guided us. Often small incidents or meetings become the hinges on which our lives are determined. Some may consider them to be no more than coincidences—that we were at certain places at certain times. However, people of faith see these as the providence of God. The Lord reminded David that He had been **with** David wherever he went. God had defeated his **enemies.** He had given David **a great name.** (The NIV understands this last statement to be part of God's promises concerning the future. It reads: "Now I will make your name great." The NRSV and the NASB also follow this view.) This was amazing! A small nation in a world of superpowers had a king known far and wide.

But what God had done for David in the past was small by comparison to what He would do for him in the future. The people of Israel already lived in the promised land, but God pointed to a time when they would be planted there in a way never again to be afflicted by **the children of wickedness.** They had been under attack since the time of the **judges,** but God promised a time of **rest from all thine enemies.** But the greatest promise, and the key to the other promises for the future, was God's words to David that God would make David **an house.**

Earlier, David had expressed his desire to build God a house or building as a place of worship. God now promised to make a **house** for David, but God was not speaking of a building. **House** translates *bayit,* which can refer to a building, a household, a family, or a dynasty.

The last part of verse 11 emphasizes that the Lord will bring this to pass: "The LORD declares to you that the LORD himself will establish a house for you" (NIV).

2 Samuel 7:12-16: **And when thy days be fulfilled, and thou shalt sleep with thy fathers, I will set up thy seed after thee, which shall proceed out of thy bowels, and I will establish his kingdom. [13]He shall build an house for my name, and I will establish the throne of his kingdom forever. [14]I will be his father, and he shall be my son. If he commit iniquity, I will chasten him with the rod of men, and with the stripes of the children of men: [15]but my mercy shall not depart away from him, as I took it from Saul, whom I put away before thee. [16]And thine house and thy kingdom shall be established forever before thee: thy throne shall be established forever.**

God's promise to David was to be fulfilled after David's death, which is described in two ways typical of the Old Testament: **When thy days be fulfilled, and thou shalt sleep with thy fathers.** Although the word *covenant* is not used in this passage, it is used in verses such as 2 Samuel 23:5 and Psalm 89:3, which refer to this promise. David and those who followed him saw this promise as a divine covenant.

God began by telling David that He would establish his **seed** in his kingdom. The most immediate fulfillment of this was the establishment of David's heir to the throne of Israel as the new king. This was fulfilled in the establishment of Solomon as king. We know this because it was Solomon whom the Lord allowed to **build an house for** the Lord's **name.** This of course was the famous temple of Solomon. Since God's **name** refers to God's presence, the temple signified the presence of God with Israel. Yet in Solomon's prayer of dedication, he recognized that no building could contain the Lord God, Creator of heaven and earth (1 Kings 8:27).

The new word in verse 13 is **forever.** Promising the kingdom to David's son is one thing; promising that this kingdom will last forever is something more. Solomon, like David, was mortal. No matter how grand was his reign, he would die. How then could his kingdom last forever? Obviously, **seed** referred to more than one generation of David's descendants. The word **seed** could refer to one descendant or to many. As it happened, there were many generations of David's offspring who lived and died before the coming of the one King whose kingdom is forever. But for most of the people of the Old Testament, they understood this to mean that an earthly descendant of David would always reign over Israel.

Verse 15 shows that one of the meanings of the promise was that the kingdom of Israel was always to be ruled by one of David's descendants. Unlike Saul, who left no son to reign after him, David would have an unbroken succession. On a purely earthly level this kept a descendant of David as ruler of the kingdom until the fall of Judah. After the kingdom of Israel divided, the Northern Kingdom had a series of different dynasties as their kings; however, the Southern Kingdom had only descendants of David. Although some of these were evil rulers, they were of David's line.

God said of the seed of David, **I will be his father, and he shall be my son.** The rest of verse 14 shows that the immediate reference was to Solomon. He did **commit iniquity,** and God did **chasten him.**

God's promise was based on what God had done, was doing, and would do. The word translated **mercy** ("love," NIV; "lovingkindness," NASB; "steadfast love," NRSV) is *hesed.* This is a key word in the Old Testament because it refers to the central character of the Lord. It occurs twice in Exodus 34:6-7, "the John 3:16 of the Old Testament." The word refers to God's covenant love and faithfulness.

What lasting truths are in these verses?

1. God made a special promise to David but a promise from which all Christians benefit.

2. The fulfillment of the promise is based on the faithful love of God, not on the faithfulness of David or of his heirs.

3. The fulfillment of God's promises to us is based not on human strength but on divine power.

A Reason to Hope (Ps. 89:1-4)

What two related words describe God? What two terms describe David? How did the covenant with David become the basis of the hope of a Messiah? How does confident hope in God enable believers to endure the worst of times?

Psalm 89:1-4: I will sing of the mercies of the LORD forever: with my mouth will I make known thy faithfulness to all generations. ²For I have said, Mercy shall be built up forever; thy faithfulness shalt thou establish in the very heavens. ³I have made a covenant with my chosen, I have sworn unto David my servant, ⁴Thy seed will I establish forever, and build up thy throne to all generations. Selah.

Psalm 89 clearly shows that the covenant with David became the basis for the hope of the Messiah in Israel. Their basic response was praise and gratitude to God for this promise. The true language of faith is praise and thanksgiving, and singing is a basic form of such worship. Thus the psalmist wrote, **I will sing of the mercies of the LORD forever.** Verse 1 is an example of synonymous parallelism in Hebrew poetry. Each half of the verse makes the same basic point but in different words. Parallel to **sing** is **with my mouth will I make known.** Parallel to **the mercies of the LORD** is **thy faithfulness.** Parallel to **forever** is **to all generations.**

Mercies is another use of *hesed*. **Faithfulness** is a companion word, *'emuna*, which appears seven times throughout Psalm 89 (vv. 1,2,5,8,24,33,49). This is obviously a key word in this psalm. *Hesed* occurs over 100 times in the Book of Psalms. The covenant with David and all divine promises are based on God's covenant love and faithfulness. The same two words occur together again in verse 2. This is the basis for the confident hope of believers.

Verses 1-2 are the words of the psalmist as a typical believer. Verses 3-4 are the words spoken by God. Although the word **covenant** is not found in 2 Samuel 7:8-16, it is found in Psalm 89:3 in connection with God's promise to David. **David** is referred to in verse 3 as God's **servant** and His **chosen.** Verse 4 essentially reinforces the heart of the covenant promise from 2 Samuel 7. Four key words from 2 Samuel are repeated in verse 4. The promises involved David's **seed.** God promised to **establish** the **throne** of David **to all generations,** or forever.

Psalm 89 is usually classified as one of the Royal Psalms. Commenting on these psalms, one Bible student wrote many years ago: "In the light of outer circumstances, this confidence in the future sway of a Jewish Messiah was a piece of absurd audacity. Assyria, Babylon, and Egypt, the great world powers with which Israel had to do, were mighty empires whose architecture even in its ruins well-nigh takes away our breath. The Jewish people, on the other hand, were a simple shepherd folk, occupying a narrow neck of land, much of it little more than piles of volcanic rock."[2]

When you read the entire psalm, you find that the final section begins with "but" (v. 38) and proceeds to describe a situation that seems to disprove the promise to David. Bible students do not know for sure which of the many crises faced by Israel was in the mind of the psalmist; however, the principle applies to any crisis that seems to cast doubt on the fact that the Lord knows and cares for His people. The greatest test for the Israelites came after their nation was defeated and they were carried into exile. For centuries there was no throne of David and no king of Israel. During those years the hope for the Messiah was tested. A faithful remnant clung to their confident hope that God would fulfill His promises in His own time and way.

One of the best biblical examples of this persevering faith and hope is the prophet Habakkuk, who prophesied about the time of the Babylonian invasion and the downfall of the Davidic kingdom of Judah. Habakkuk's final response is faith and hope at its best.

> Fig trees may no longer bloom,
>> or vineyards produce grapes;
> olive trees may be fruitless,
>> and harvest time a failure;
> sheep pens may be empty,
>> and cattle stalls vacant—
> but I will still celebrate
>> because the LORD God saves me (Hab. 3:17-18, CEV).

What are the lasting lessons of these verses?

1. Sing praises to the Lord for His lovingkindness and faithfulness.
2. Maintain your confident hope in spite of difficult circumstances.

A Ruler to Come (Isa. 9:6-7)

Why did many Jews look for an earthly Messiah-King? What kind of Messiah-King did Isaiah describe in these verses? What words did Isaiah use to describe the One for whom he hoped? What Bible examples of the birth of a child heralded significant stages in God's redemptive plan? What was the ultimate fulfillment of Isaiah's prophecy in 9:6-7? How should we acknowledge the kingship and lordship of Jesus Christ?

Isaiah 9:6-7: For unto us a child is born, unto us a son is given: and the government shall be upon his shoulder: and his name shall be called Wonderful, Counselor, The mighty God, The everlasting Father, The Prince of Peace. ⁷Of the increase of his government and peace there shall be no end, upon the throne of David, and upon his kingdom, to order it, and to establish it with judgment and with justice from henceforth even forever. The zeal of the LORD of hosts will perform this.

The covenant with David thus became the basis for the hope for a Messiah. Many of the Old Testament people of God expected an earthly king of David's line who would defeat the enemies of Israel and restore the nation's former grandeur. This same earthly hope prevailed even in the time of Jesus. As a prophet, Isaiah may have passed through a stage when he expected one of Israel's kings of David's line to be the Messiah. Some believe that he may have had such hopes for Hezekiah, one of Judah's better kings. However, by the time Isaiah wrote 9:6-7 he had moved beyond such an expectation. He still expected the Messiah to be **born** and live as a **child,** but he saw this One in terms of many titles, some of which are clearly divine titles.

In the Bible, God often began some new phase of His work with the birth of a child. Isaac was the child of promise born to Abraham and Sarah in their old age. Moses was divinely spared from Pharaoh's order to have boy babies of the Hebrews killed. Samuel was born in answer to the fervent prayers of his barren mother Hannah. John the Baptist was born to the aged couple Zachariah and Elisabeth. Jesus was conceived by the Holy Spirit in the virgin Mary. Christians believe that the ultimate fulfillment of Isaiah 9:6-7 is in Jesus the Messiah-King. The child of Isaiah 9:6-7 is the same child described in Isaiah 7:14 as born of a virgin and called "Immanuel." Although Isaiah 9:6-7 is not directly quoted in the New Testament (although it may be alluded to in Luke 1:32-33), there is no doubt that the believers saw Jesus as the fulfillment of this prophecy.

This conclusion is supported by many things found in the text of Isaiah 9:6-7. The **child** is also called a **son.** The words **is given** reflect the New Testament emphasis on Jesus as given by God to save sinful humanity. The four titles of this One depict someone who is more than human. (In the *King James Version* there are five titles, but most translators remove the comma after **Wonderful.** This makes four titles of two words each.)

Wonderful, Counselor emphasizes two qualities of the King. He is Himself a wonder, and He is a wise Counselor and Guide. Wisdom was highly prized in ancient society. Wisdom was more than knowledge; it was insight into natural and supernatural realities. **Mighty God** is surely a divine title. "By means of the words *yeled,* **child,** and *yullad,* **is born,** he [the inspired prophet] has called attention to the Messiah's humanity, but by the phrase *'el gibbor* we are brought face to face with Messiah's deity."[3] **Everlasting Father** points to two realities about God. He is the eternal God who created and sustains all things, and He is the loving Father of His children. **Prince of Peace** is a royal figure who is the very embodiment of peace. When Jesus was born, angels spoke of His bringing peace (Luke 2:14). He brings to sinners peace with God as they are reconciled to God through the shed blood of Jesus (Rom. 5:1; Eph. 2:17). He brings the ideal of peace among different groups of believers (Eph. 2:14). He gives believers an inner peace that defies human understanding (Phil. 4:7). Some day He will bring peace to a strife-torn world (Isa. 2:4).

The government shall be upon his shoulder is explained in verse 7. Isaiah saw this One as the descendant of David who would fulfill the promises to David. He will reign **upon the throne of David,** will **establish** a just **kingdom,** and **of his government . . . there shall be no end.** These words reflect the promises of 2 Samuel 7. This prophecy carries those promises a significant step beyond the original promises to David. This Ruler is not just another one of the kings of David's line who would reign over Judah. This One is the divine Son who establishes the kingdom forever.

The kingdom will be characterized by **peace** *(shalom),* **judgment** *(mispat,* "justice," NIV), and **justice** *(sᵉdaqa,* "righteousness," NIV). These qualities are ensured by the nature of the One who rules as

The Prince of Peace. He is the epitome of justice and righteousness. During His earthly ministry Jesus displayed these qualities. These same qualities will be displayed in His future reign. Those who know Him should live now by the standards of this coming kingdom.

What assurance did Isaiah have that these promises would be fulfilled? **The zeal of the LORD of hosts will perform this.** The fulfillment of this promise is not dependent on us but on the Lord. He can and will do what is impossible for human beings.

What are the lasting lessons in these verses?

1. The covenant with David has been fulfilled in the coming of Jesus Christ, the son of David and the Son of God.

2. Christ's kingdom is everlasting.

3. Believers should follow Christ as Lord of their lives.

❖ *Spiritual Transformations*

When David wanted to build a house for worshiping God, God promised to build David a house (a dynasty) that would last forever. This became the basis for the hope of the Messiah-King, a confident hope that enabled the Jews to pass through many hard times. The ultimate fulfillment of the messianic hope was not an earthly king but the eternal Son of God.

Three basic applications grow out of these passages: (1) Depend on the Lord to fulfill His promises. (2) Cling to confident hope in God even when things are at their worst. (3) In all things, honor and obey Jesus Christ as Lord.

Which of these applications do you need to emphasize in your life?

_____

What actions do you need to take to make this application?

_____

Prayer of Commitment: Almighty God, help me to trust in Your promises, to rely on You in hard times, and to honor Christ as Lord at all times. Amen.

---

[1]Joyce G. Baldwin, *1 and 2 Samuel*, in the Tyndale Old Testament Commentaries [Downers Grove: InterVarsity Press, 1988], 214.

[2]Rollin H. Walker, *The Modern Message of the Psalms* [Nashville: Abingdon-Cokesbury Press, 1938], 172.

[3]Edward J. Young, *The Book of Isaiah*, vol. 1, second edition [Grand Rapids: William B. Eerdmans Publishing Company, 1972], 337.

Study Theme

Entering into a Covenant of Grace with God

Concerning the Epistle to the Romans, Leon Morris wrote, "It is commonly agreed that the Epistle to the Romans is one of the greatest Christian writings. Its power has been demonstrated again and again at critical points in the history of the Christian church. Augustine of Hippo, for example, was converted through reading a passage from this letter, and thus began a period of the greatest importance for the church. It is not too much to say that at a later time Martin Luther's spiritual experience was shaped by his coming to grips with what Paul says in this epistle. The Reformation may be regarded as the unleashing of a new spiritual life as a result of a renewed understanding of the teaching of Romans. Again, John Wesley's conversion was triggered by hearing Luther's Preface to Romans read, a Preface, of course, inspired by the epistle. . . . But Romans is not for great minds only. The humble believer also finds inspiration and direction in these pages. Romans is not an easy book. But it has always yielded rich dividends to anyone who has taken the time to study it seriously, and it does so still."[1]

In this four-session Study Theme we will be focusing on some key passages from this powerful letter Paul wrote to the Roman believers. The first lesson, "Everyone Needs Salvation," is based on Romans 1:14-20; 2:17-24. This lesson has a missionary message based on passages that show the universal reality of sin. The second lesson, "Salvation Is Available," is an evangelistic lesson based on Romans 3:19-30. The third lesson, "Salvation Means a New Life," is based on Romans 5:1-11,18-21. This lesson looks at the fruits of being declared righteous by God. The fourth lesson, "Salvation Begins a Life of Obedience," is based on Romans 6:12-23. This lesson refutes the false idea that being saved is the end of salvation, not the beginning of a new life of obedience to God.

[1] Leon Morris, *The Epistle to the Romans* [Grand Rapids: William B. Eerdmans Publishing Company, 1998], 1.

EVERYONE NEEDS SALVATION

Background Passage: Romans 1:8-20; 2:17-24
Focal Passage: Romans 1:14-20; 2:17-24
Key Verse: Romans 1:16

❖ *Significance of the Lesson*

• The *Theme* of this lesson is that everyone needs to be saved.
• The *Life Question* this lesson seeks to address is, Who needs to be saved?
• The *Biblical Truth* is that all people need salvation because they are sinners.
• The *Life Impact* is to help you have a burden for the salvation of lost people that compels you to witness.

Me, a Sinner?

In a secular worldview, many adults find it hard to believe that they are sinners deserving God's wrath and needing salvation. Some acknowledge that sin is in the world, but not in their lives. Other adults admit that sin is in their lives, but they do not consider it to be a serious problem. Still others know that it is a serious problem, but they don't know what to do about it. Too many professed Christians show no concern about the plight of lost people. In a world of permissiveness, many believe that one's actions are just matters of personal choice.

In the biblical worldview, all are sinners and sin is a deadly plight from which people cannot set themselves free. Sinners stand under the wrath of God, but God desires that none perish and that all come to salvation through faith in Jesus Christ. Those who experience salvation have an obligation to share the good news with those who are lost.

Word Study: *Salvation*

The Greek word for **salvation** is *soteria*. It is related to the verb for "save," *sozo*, and the noun "Savior," *soter*. *Soteria* was used by the Greeks to describe deliverance from some threat or danger and at times to describe the result of that deliverance. This common word was used in the same ways in the New Testament, except that the deliverance normally was from sin and spiritual death through Jesus the Savior. The verb and the noun show that salvation was a past experience of deliverance from the guilt of sin, present salvation from the power of sin, and future salvation from the presence of sin. All aspects of God's salvation are by God's grace through faith in Jesus.

❖ *Search the Scriptures*

Paul wrote that he was obligated by his own experience of salvation to tell the good news of salvation to all people. He summarized the provision God has made for the salvation of all people. He described the terrible sins of the ungodly Gentiles as evidence of their need for the good news. Then Paul showed that the Jewish people also are sinners who need the good news.

Concern for All People (Rom. 1:14-15)

How do these verses fit into Paul's introduction? In what sense was Paul a **debtor***? Who were his creditors? To what degree was he committed to paying that debt? Why did Paul want to go to Rome?*

1:14-15: I am debtor both to the Greeks, and to the Barbarians; both to the wise, and to the unwise. [15]So, as much as in me is, I am ready to preach the gospel to you that are at Rome also.

Paul began his letter with a typical salutation (1:1-7). He expressed appreciation for the faith of the Roman believers and told of his long-held desire to preach at Rome (vv. 8-13). Romans 15:20-33 gives more details about Paul's situation when he wrote the letter and his plans to visit Rome. He was headed for Jerusalem with an offering he had received from the Gentile churches. Paul knew that this was a dangerous mission; therefore, he asked the Romans to pray for the success of this crucial mission. He said that after that mission, he hoped to come to Rome, spend time with them, and then go on to Spain.

In explaining why he went to so many different places with the good news, Paul wrote that he considered himself a **debtor.** He used the normal Greek word for someone who owes a debt to someone else. Paul's reasoning was like this. He had received the salvation of God for his many sins through the good news of Jesus Christ. The world was filled with people who were in sin as he once was. He felt obligated to see that they had the same opportunity to be saved. Of this sense of obligation, Paul elsewhere wrote, "For though I preach the gospel, I have nothing to glory of: for necessity is laid upon me; yea, woe is unto me, if I preach not the gospel!" (1 Cor. 9:16).

To whom did Paul owe this debt? He wrote that he owed it **to the Greeks, and to the Barbarians; both to the wise, and to the unwise. Greeks** refers to actual Greeks and to those who spoke the Greek language, which was just about everyone in the Roman Empire. The conquests of Alexander the Great had spread the Greek language and culture far and wide. **Barbarians** were those who did not speak Greek. The Greek word *barbaros* describes how these people sounded to the Greeks. They sounded as if they were saying, "bar, bar, bar." Thus these two categories included everyone. The **wise** and the **unwise** refers to people of different educational levels. This also includes everyone. Since God is not willing for anyone to perish, Paul was committed to tell the good news to everyone whom he could reach with the message.

He did not do this reluctantly but eagerly and joyfully. The word **ready** can be translated "eager" (NIV). What is the meaning of the words **as much as in me is**? These words refer to Paul's personal willingness to do what the Lord wills to be done. It is like saying that he was totally committed to do his part in telling the good news. His real debt of love was owed to the Lord, and telling the good news to others could pay this debt.

> But drops of grief can ne'er repay
> The debt of love I owe;
> Here, Lord, I give myself away,
> 'Tis all that I can do.[1]

At the same time, love for the Lord is expressed in love for others. Paul felt that he owed to all people the opportunity to know the salvation he had experienced. Suppose a researcher found the cure for cancer or some other dreaded disease. What kind of person would keep that knowledge to himself or herself? You will probably say that only a crazy person would not want to reap the enormous financial benefits of this discovery. But suppose there was no financial pay-off. What kind of person would know the cure for cancer and not share it with those who are sick? Paul felt that he had found the cure for a far more deadly disease than cancer, and he felt obligated to tell the good news to all people, for all had the disease.

The word **gospel** in Greek is *euangelizo*, which means "to tell good news." Most of us cannot keep good news to ourselves. When something good happens to us, we want to share it with others. If the good news involves benefiting others, we have further motivation to tell the good news.

What lasting truths are in these verses?

1. People who have experienced salvation have an obligation to share the good news with all people.

2. All people need this good news.

Provision for All (Rom. 1:16-17)

*What might cause someone to be **ashamed of the gospel of Christ** in first-century Rome? What shows that Paul was **not ashamed**? How is **the power of God** related to **salvation**? What is the significance of the last part of verse 17?*

1:16-17: For I am not ashamed of the gospel of Christ: for it is the power of God unto salvation to everyone that believeth; to the Jew first, and also to the Greek. ¹⁷For therein is the righteousness of God revealed from faith to faith: as it is written, The just shall live by faith.

The Christian gospel was foolishness to the Greeks and a stumbling block to the Jews (1 Cor. 1:18-25). Courage was needed to preach the gospel in such a world. We think of Paul as almost super-human, but he was only human. He asked the churches to pray that he might speak the word boldly (Eph. 6:18-20). When he arrived in Rome, he preached boldly to the Jews (Acts 28:17-31). Because he was under house arrest, he was chained to Roman soldiers. Yet Paul witnessed to them (Phil. 1:12-13). Truly he was **not ashamed of the gospel of Christ.** Or as the *Contemporary English Version* renders it in a positive way, "I am proud of the good news!"

Power translates *dynamis*, from which we get our word *dynamite*. Some people excuse their rejection of Christ by saying, "I can't live the Christian life." This is true. None of us can—in our own strength. Being saved, however, opens our lives to the presence and power of the Spirit of the Lord. He provides the power to set us free from sin and to overcome it in daily life.

This **salvation** is available **to everyone that believeth; to the Jew first, and also to the Greek.** Just as all need the good news, all can receive it by grace through faith. The Greeks divided humanity into themselves and the Barbarians. The Jews divided humanity into themselves and the Greeks, or Gentiles.

Verse 17 states what probably is the theme of Romans—**the righteousness of God. Righteousness** is *dikaiosune.* It is related to the word **just** ("righteous," NIV), which is *dikaios,* and to the word *justify, dikaioo,* which plays such a vital role in Romans. There is considerable discussion about what Paul meant by **the righteousness of God.** Some see it as only an attribute of God, but the word *dikaioo* shows that it is also the saving activity of declaring sinners right with God through their faith in Christ.

One thing is clear. Paul denied that human righteousness could save us. Only God's righteousness saves. The reason our righteousness cannot save is that the only righteousness apart from Christ is self-righteousness, which itself is one of humanity's most deadly and deceitful sins. Paul wrote, "There is none righteous, no, not one" (3:10). "By nature we view righteousness as something we can achieve by our own meritorious action, the result of what we do. The righteousness of God is totally different. It is a right standing before God that has nothing to do with human merit. It is received by faith."[2]

Paul quoted Habakkuk 2:4 in verse 17: **The just** ("righteous," NIV) **shall live by faith.** This was the verse that opened the windows of heaven for Martin Luther. Like Paul, he had been taught that salvation is based on merit or good works. Luther, however, found no release from his guilt by his good works. He studied Galatians and Romans, and these words made the difference. Formerly Luther had thought of **the righteousness of God** only as God's justice demanding punishment for human sins. Luther wrote: "Night and day I pondered until I saw the connection between the justice of God and the statement that 'the just shall live by his faith.' Then I grasped that the justice of God is that righteousness by which through grace and sheer mercy God justifies us through faith. Thereupon I felt myself to be reborn and to have gone through open doors into paradise. The whole of Scripture took on new meaning. . . ."[3]

What are the lasting truths in these verses?

1. Don't be ashamed of the gospel of Christ.

2. The power of God makes salvation possible.

3. "The righteousness of God" refers not only to an attribute of God but also to His actions in providing salvation for sinners.

4. No one can be saved by good works, but only by the grace of God.

Need of All: Godless People (Rom. 1:18-20)

*What is **the wrath of God**? What were the sins of the Gentile world of the first century? Why are all people **without excuse**?*

1:18: For the wrath of God is revealed from heaven against all ungodliness and unrighteousness of men, who hold the truth in unrighteousness.

Much confusion exists about the meaning of **the wrath of God.** Many people deny that a God of love ever acts in wrath. Others at the opposite extreme live in constant fear of an angry God. The first group has sentimentalized love. God has both wrath and love. Both groups think of the wrath of God as a divine temper tantrum or an outburst of divine rage. However, **wrath** *(orge)* refers to God's steady and fixed opposition to sin and evil. All stand under divine wrath because all have sinned; however, God's love seeks to lead sinners to forgiveness and new life.

Another point of confusion about wrath is when it becomes effective. Closely related is whether it is the working out of a law of sin and retribution or God's personal wrath. Notice that verse 18 uses the words **is revealed.** So in some sense God's wrath is at work in the present. Yet verses such as Romans 2:5,7-8 refer to God's wrath in the future. Like many realities, wrath is both present and future.

Read Romans 1:21-32 to see how God's wrath works in individual lives and in human society. Notice the words "gave them up (over)" in verses 24,26,28. These key verses show how God allowed sinners to reap what they sowed. The result was immoral perversion and social chaos. In first-century society homosexuality became popular and social chaos was common. These sins were evidences of the wrath of God allowing the people of that day to reap the harvest of their own sinful choices. However, both the present and future wrath of God is God's personal wrath, not just the working out of some impersonal law built into the fabric of the universe.

The sins against which God's wrath is directed are **ungodliness and unrighteousness of men.** Their sin is also that they **hold the truth in unrighteousness. Hold** has the idea of "suppress" (NKJV, NIV, NASB, NRSV). That is, although God reveals truth to them, they reject it. Verses 19-20 show the consequences of this refusal of God's revelation.

1:19-20: **Because that which may be known of God is manifest in them; for God hath showed it unto them. ²⁰For the invisible things of him from the creation of the world are clearly seen, being understood by the things that are made, even his eternal power and Godhead; so that they are without excuse.**

Most of verses 19-20 refer to God's revelation to all humanity in His created works and to the human choice to reject this revelation. Theologians speak of "natural revelation" as God's revelation of Himself in His creation (see Ps. 19:1). This kind of revelation is not as clear as "special revelation" through the words and events of the Scriptures; however, God's **eternal power and Godhead** ("divine nature," NIV) . . . **are clearly seen.** The revelation is clear enough that those who reject it **are without excuse.**

What are the lasting truths in these verses?

1. The wrath of God is a present and a future reality.

2. God has revealed Himself in nature, but people have rejected Him.

3. Because each has had an opportunity to know God, each is without excuse.

Need of All: Religious People (Rom. 2:17-24)

How is Romans 1–2 similar in approach to Amos 1–2? Why were Jews as well as Gentiles without excuse? What claims did the Jews make for their relation to God? What probing questions did Paul ask his fellow Jews? What serious charge did he make in verse 24? How do these truths relate to religious people other than the Jews?

2:17-20: **Behold, thou art called a Jew, and restest in the law, and makest thy boast of God, ¹⁸and knowest his will, and approvest the things that are more excellent, being instructed out of the law; ¹⁹and art confident that thou thyself art a guide of the blind, a light of them which are in darkness, ²⁰an instructor of the foolish, a teacher of babes, which hast the form of knowledge and of the truth in the law.**

Romans 1–2 has something in common with Amos 1–2. When the prophet Amos began his preaching, he began with the sins of other nations. The Israelite audience probably was saying "amen" to all of these words of condemnation of rival and enemy nations. Then Amos turned his attention to the sins of Israel, and the people were less ready to face their own sins. This was Paul's strategy. In showing that all were sinners, he began with the terrible sins of the pagan world (1:18-32). It is a grim list of sins that he described. The records of that day confirm the truth of Paul's account of the sins of the pagan world. Then in chapter 2, Paul turned to the sins of the Jews.

Paul began by saying that those who judged the sins of others were themselves without excuse (2:1). He further developed this theme in verses 1-16. Then he addressed himself directly to the **Jew.** Verses 17-20 consists of a series of four clauses, the first of which begins with the Greek word for "if." The same word is assumed to precede all four clauses. The *New International Version* clarifies this: "If you call yourself a Jew; if you rely on the law and brag about your relationship to God; if you know his will and approve of what is superior because you are instructed by the law; if you are convinced that you are a guide for the blind, a light for those who are in the dark, an instructor of the foolish, a teacher of infants, because you have in the law the embodiment of knowledge and truth. . . ." As you see, in Greek this is not really a complete sentence until verse 21 is added. However, these four clauses focus on some basic claims by first-century Jews.

The key word in these verses is **law.** For the Jews, all of their distinctive claims were based on the fact that as God's chosen people, God had given them His special revelation in the law. The only revelation that pagans had was the revelation of God in nature. This is not so clear and strong as the revelation of God in words and events. From Paul's point of view, this only made the Jews that much more accountable to God. However, for many Jews the law was used as a basis for pride and self-righteousness. The Jews considered themselves morally superior to the Gentiles, and often they were; however, pride and self-righteousness are among the most deceitful and deadly sins. Nothing keeps someone from the grace of God so much as self-righteousness. No one knew this better than Paul, for he had once felt the same way until he met the Lord Jesus on the Damascus road. Then he saw the depth of his own sins.

2:21-24: **Thou therefore which teachest another, teachest thou not thyself? thou that preachest a man should not steal, dost thou steal? [22]Thou that sayest a man should not commit adultery, dost thou commit adultery? thou that abhorrest idols, dost thou commit sacrilege? [23]Thou that makest thy boast of the law, through breaking the law dishonorest thou God? [24]For the name of God is blasphemed among the Gentiles through you, as it is written.**

Paul attacked these proud claims of his fellow Jews with some probing questions. In verse 21 he asked if they practiced what they professed, taught, and preached. Then he became specific. The Jews followed the Eighth Commandment in condemning stealing. Paul asked, "Do you steal?" (NIV). Paul asked the same question about the Seventh Commandment. They preached against adultery. Paul asked, "Do you commit adultery?" (NIV). The test of loyalty is not how loudly one thunders about this sin; the real test is one's own practice. The Jews abhorred idolatry. Paul asked them how many had committed **sacrilege.** Most translators believe this refers to robbing temples (NKJV, NIV, NASB, NRSV). Others believe that Paul had in mind the more general sin of sacrilegious behavior.

Paul ended the questions with verse 23. Then he made a direct accusation against the Jews as a group. Quoting from Isaiah 52:5, Paul accused his generation of Jews with actions that led to **the name of God** being **blasphemed among the Gentiles.** By their inconsistency and hypocrisy they had held the name of their God up to ridicule among unbelievers.

Many non-Christians use the excuse of hypocrites in the church. We know that no one can hide behind an excuse, but who can deny that the behavior of many professing Christians is often inconsistent and sometimes downright hypocritical?

What are the lasting truths in these verses?

1. Pride and self-righteousness are deceitful sins.

2. Those who have the revelation of God in His Word are more accountable than those who have only God's revelation in nature.

3. God will judge us not by what we claim but by what we do.

4. Inconsistent and hypocritical actions by religious people encourage nonbelievers to blaspheme the name of God.

❖ *Spiritual Transformations*

Paul considered himself a debtor with an obligation to tell the good news to all people. This was based on the fact that all had sinned and needed the good news and based on Paul's own experience of salvation through faith in Jesus Christ. Paul wrote of the righteousness of God in offering salvation for sinners and the wrath of God in punishing sinners.

Two strong motivations for missions and evangelism are in this lesson. One is the deadly plight of those in sin, and the other is the Christian's own experience of salvation by God's grace through faith. Each believer should feel obligated to share the good news with all people.

Within a few weeks most churches will be emphasizing international missions. *What is your part in international missions?* _____

_____

To what degree do you feel obligated to share the good news of Christ with people you know? _____

Prayer of Commitment: Lord, help me fulfill my obligation to share the good news with all people. Amen.

[1] Isaac Watts, "At the Cross," No. 139, *The Baptist Hymnal,* 1991.

[2] Robert H. Mounce, "Romans," in *The New American Commentary,* vol. 27 [Nashville: Broadman & Holman Publishers, 1995], 73.

[3] Quoted by Roland H. Bainton, *Here I Stand: A Life of Martin Luther* [New York: The New American Library, 1950], 49-50.

Week of November 10

SALVATION IS AVAILABLE

Bible Passage: Romans 3:19-30
Key Verses: Romans 3:23-24

❖ *Significance of the Lesson*

• The *Theme* of this lesson is that salvation is available to all through faith in Jesus Christ.
• The *Life Question* this lesson seeks to address is, How can I be saved?
• The *Biblical Truth* is that those who put their faith in Jesus Christ receive salvation.
• The *Life Impact* is to help you receive salvation through faith in Jesus Christ.
• This is the *Evangelism Lesson* for this quarter.

How to Be Saved

In the secular worldview, many are indifferent to being right with God. Many believe that if there is a God and a heaven, everyone will go there. Those who are concerned believe that they can be acceptable to God if they live a decent, moral life.

In the biblical worldview, all have sinned and no one can be good enough to be acceptable to God. God sent Jesus to die for human sins and to bear in His own body the sins of the world. Through faith in Him sinners can be declared right with God.

Word Study: *Justify*

The Greek word *dikaioo* is translated "justify" or "declare righteous." This key word is found five times in Romans 3:19-31 (vv. 20,24,26,28,30). This was a key word in the difference between Paul's view of how to be declared right by God before and after he met Jesus Christ. Before he met the Lord, he shared the belief of most first-century Jews and most people in every age, which holds that people make themselves acceptable to God by their good lives. The Pharisees taught that people would be justified by God at the day of judgment based on their good works. Paul taught that sinners can be declared righteous by God at the time they trust Jesus Christ as their Savior.

Other words from the same root appear in the Focal Passage. The righteousness *(dikaiosune)* of God is referred to in verses 21,22,25,26. The adjective "righteous" or "just" *(dikaios)* is found in verse 26. This crucial verse contains all three of these words.

❖ *Search the Scriptures*

Good works cannot save us because all are guilty of sin. God provides the way of salvation by His grace through faith in Jesus Christ. The atoning death of Jesus Christ shows that God is both just and the justifier of believing sinners. All human boasting and pride are out of place. God offers justification by faith to Jews and to Gentiles.

Works Can't Save Us (Rom. 3:19-21)

*In what sense is **every mouth . . . stopped**? Why can no one be justified **by the deeds of the law**? How do **the law and the prophets** bear witness to the universal reality of human sin?*

Verses 19-20: Now we know that what things soever the law saith, it saith to them who are under the law: that every mouth may be stopped, and all the world may become guilty before God. ²⁰Therefore by the deeds of the law there shall no flesh be justified in his sight: for by the law is the knowledge of sin.

Paul had been demonstrating that both Gentiles and Jews are sinners who have no excuse for their sins because each rejected God's revelation to them. Gentiles had rejected God's revelation in His creation (1:18-32; especially v. 20). Jews had rejected God's revelation in His revealed law (2:1–3:8; especially 2:1). In 3:9-18 Paul quoted a string of Old Testament verses showing the sinfulness of Jews and Gentiles. Verse 19 sums up this idea of all people being without excuse.

Verse 19 seems directed primarily to Paul's Jewish readers, from whom he had received most criticism. Pharisaic Jews claimed acceptance by God based on faithfully keeping **the law** that God had given Israel. Paul insisted that the problem with that view was that no one perfectly obeyed their law. They were **under the law** but **by the deeds of the law there shall no flesh be justified in his sight.** They could not be made acceptable by keeping the law, for the law itself condemned them of their sins. The law could not save from sin; instead, it brought **the knowledge of sin** (see also Gal. 3:19-24). For those such as Paul, who tried to keep the law, honesty compelled them to recognize in the law's demands that they had broken God's law.

The result of this conviction of sin by the law itself had this result, which Paul stated in two different ways in verse 19. First, **every mouth may be stopped** ("silenced," NIV; "so that no one may have anything to say in self-defence," REB, NEB). Robert Mounce commented of this clause that it "pictures a defendant in court rendered speechless by the evidence brought against him."[1] This is an appropriate way to describe this analogy from a court of law, since the whole idea of justification is drawn from this setting. People come before God's bar of justice. The evidence is against them in an overwhelming way. On their own, they have no hope of being declared innocent. The second way of describing the result of the law's condemnation of those who rely on it for their acceptance by God is in the words **and all the world may become guilty before God. Guilty** is a term from the law court. Sinners could not be declared innocent based on their actions, for the evidence showed that they were guilty. "The image, then, is of all humanity standing before God, accountable to him for willful and inexcusable violations of his will, awaiting the sentence of condemnation that their actions deserve."[2]

This was Paul's answer to those who claimed that God would accept them on the day of judgment based on the evidence of their obedience to His law. The problem with this deceptive hope was that the evidence did not prove their innocence but their guilt.

Verse 21: **But now the righteousness of God without the law is manifested, being witnessed by the law and the prophets.**

Did this mean that the law had no value? Not at all. In addition to showing people their sins, **the law and the prophets** revealed **the righteousness of God without** ("apart from," NIV) **the law.** Both Paul and his critics sought to base their positions on the Old Testament. The Hebrew Scriptures had three divisions: Law, Prophets (which includes some books we call "history"), and Writings. All three divisions are mentioned in Luke 24:44. When referring to Scripture, the word **law** *(nomos)* usually refers to the Mosaic Law in the first five books of the Hebrew Bible. At times, **law** stands for all three divisions of the Old Testament. This is the case in verse 19, which follows a string of quotations from Psalms (the largest book in the Writings) and the Prophets. The phrase **the law and the prophets** is also sometimes used in the New Testament to refer to the Old Testament. This is the case in verse 21.

What are the lasting truths in verses 19-21?

1. The evidence in the Scriptures of the universal reality of sin is so strong that it silences all excuses and every defense.

2. No one can be declared righteous based on keeping the demands of the law.

3. The law does not provide the means of salvation but shows people their sins.

4. The righteousness of God is supported in all parts of the Old Testament.

We Can Trust in Jesus (Rom. 3:22-24)

*How does faith in Jesus Christ justify sinners before God? In what sense did Paul use the words **there is no difference**? In what way is salvation free and in what sense is it costly?*

Verses 22-24: Even the righteousness of God which is by faith of Jesus Christ unto all and upon all them that believe: for there is no difference: [23]for all have sinned, and come short of the glory of God; [24]being justified freely by his grace through the redemption that is in Christ Jesus.

The expression **the righteousness of God** was found in 1:17 and in 3:21,22 (see also 3:25,26). Verses 22-24 emphasize that it refers primarily to God's justifying or declaring sinners righteous **by faith of** ("in," NKJV, NASB, NIV) **Jesus Christ.** Paul's critics apparently asked, "How can a person who is not righteous be declared righteous by God?" This was especially true if the person was ungodly (4:5).

Paul's answer has several points to it. One is that this is the only way that anyone can be acceptable to God. On our own, none of us is righteous enough to be declared righteous by God. Paul had spelled this out in great detail in Romans 1:18–3:20. Verse 23 sums up his conclusion, which was based on study of the Scriptures, personal experience, and observation of others—**All have sinned, and come short of the glory of God.** One meaning of the word for sin *(harmatano)* is "to miss the mark" or "to fall short." An old mountaineer was noted for being a crack shot. The basis for this reputation was targets throughout the woods showing his initials and having a bullet hole in the center of the target. Someone realized that no one had ever actually seen him shoot. Someone followed him the next time he went out to shoot. The man fired at a tree. Then he went and drew a target around the bullet hole. All of us could claim to have hit the center of God's demands if we could build His demands around our lives. However, when the Lord sets His target, we miss the mark of God's expectation.

A second reason why justification is possible only through faith in Jesus Christ is because God offers salvation based on **his grace,** not based on our good works. Jesus is the only way because He is the down-reaching arm of the God of grace. God sent His Son to live a perfect life, die an atoning death, and win victory over death. Other religions and philosophies assume that humans can make themselves acceptable to God by something they do. The good news assumes that we cannot save ourselves but that God in Christ can save us. Through placing our **faith** in Him rather than in ourselves, God can accept us on the basis of His redemptive work.

This **grace** is not earned or deserved, but is offered **freely by his grace through the redemption that is in Christ Jesus.** Salvation by God's grace is a gift of God to all who will repent of sins and trust Jesus as Lord and Savior (see 6:23). Those who accept this gift God declares righteous based on their faith in Jesus Christ.

Redemption is another word from daily life in the first century. Just as being **justified** referred to being pardoned in a court of law, **redemption** referred to the price paid for liberating a slave. In this case the price was the death of Jesus. We are redeemed by His blood (Eph. 1:7; 1 Pet. 1:18-19). Thus salvation is free yet costly. It cost God the death of His Son on the cross. This theme is developed further in Romans 3:25-26.

Because God in Christ paid the price to set sinners free, sinners are declared righteous by God based on His grace and the redemptive work of Christ, whom the sinner receives by faith. When this happens, God declares the sinner justified or righteous in His sight. The evidence shows that we are guilty without any measure of doubt. We are without excuse. We face sure conviction and punishment for our sins; however, because Jesus died for us, God offers to pardon us. And this pardon leads to a new relationship with God (5:1-8).

What are the lasting truths in verses 22-24?

1. Because all people have sinned, no one can be declared righteous based on personal goodness.

2. God offers to justify sinners based on His grace, not on human merit.

3. Salvation by grace is free to those who receive it, but salvation was purchased at the great price of the death of Jesus Christ.

God Has Provided What We Need (Rom. 3:25-26)

In what sense is Christ **a propitiation**? *How does God show that He is* **just** *when He declares sinners to be righteous?*

Verses 25-26: Whom God hath set forth to be a propitiation through faith in his blood, to declare his righteousness for the remission of sins that are past, through the forbearance of God; 26to declare, I say, at this time his righteousness: that he might be just, and the justifier of him which believeth in Jesus.

The key word in these verses is **propitiation** ("sacrifice of atonement," NIV). Christ is the propitiation *(hilasmos)* for our sins (1 John 2:2; 4:10). This rarely used English word translates the Greek word *hilasterion*, which comes from the language of sacrifice. In the Bible, God Himself set forth the sacrificial system of the Old Testament and sent His own Son to be the propitiation for our sins. People are sinners, and God is both just and merciful. By sending His Son to die for us, God Himself offered the sacrifice to satisfy His wrath toward sin and to offer mercy to sinners.

This is what Paul meant when he wrote of Christ's death as showing that God is both **just, and the justifier of him which believeth in Jesus.** This was Paul's answer to his critics who claimed that it was unjust for a just God to accept ungodly people as though they were righteous. The death of Christ thus reveals both the justice and mercy of God. The cross takes sin seriously. God had in the **past** shown **forbearance** toward sin and sinners, but He dealt with sin at the cross. Christ took upon Himself the sins of the world. He died in our place so we might not have to die. He bore the wrath that is directed toward sin.

We know from experience that forgiving a person is costly to the one who forgives. This person pays a price by absorbing the hurt and pain of the one who has sinned against him or her. God in Christ absorbed all the hurt and pain of all the sinners of all times.

Sometimes when a fire gets out of control, firefighters will use a firebreak to stop the flames from advancing. A strip of land is burned off ahead of the fire under controlled conditions. Then when the flames of the wild fire reach that area, there is nothing left to burn and the fire goes out. In a spiritual sense, Jesus has provided a firebreak for us. The judgment of God has already fallen here; therefore, in Him we are safe.

What is the lasting lesson in verses 25-26? God provided the sacrifice that satisfies the demands of justice and wrath while at the same time He offered us justification through the One who died for our sins.

Boasting Is Out of Place (Rom. 3:27-28)

*Why is human **boasting** excluded before God? How does verse 28 sum up much of the passage as a whole?*

***Verses 27-28:* Where is boasting then? It is excluded. By what law? of works? Nay: but by the law of faith. ²⁸Therefore we conclude that a man is justified by faith without the deeds of the law.**

Paul asked whether **boasting** had any place. If we were justified by our own good works or rewarded for our own righteousness, boasting would be natural. However, since no one is justified by personal righteousness but by the grace of God through faith in Christ, boasting **is excluded** (see also 1 Cor. 1:29-30; Eph. 2:8-9).

Verse 28 sums up clearly the message of the larger passage and one of the central themes of Paul's message. **Therefore** shows that Paul was stating a conclusion from what he written. Paul said, **We conclude that** people are **justified by faith without the deeds of the law.** Only a few verses later Paul wrote of God justifying the ungodly (4:5). God does not accept as righteous those who trust in and boast of their own righteousness. God does accept as righteous those who confess their sins and cast themselves on the mercy of God.

What are the lasting truths in verses 27-28?

1. No person ought to boast of personal righteousness.

2. Believers glorify God for His justification that He provides through faith in Christ.

Salvation Is for All (Rom. 3:29-30)

What was the basis for Paul's insistence that God includes **Gentiles** *as well as* **Jews** *in His salvation?*

Verses 29-30: Is he the God of the Jews only? is he not also of the Gentiles? Yes, of the Gentiles also: ³⁰seeing it is one God, which shall justify the circumcision by faith, and uncircumcision through faith.

Paul was a strong advocate for one way of salvation for all people—**Jews** (also called **the circumcision**) and **Gentiles** (also called **the uncircumcision**). He emphasized several factors in supporting his position. For one thing, all humanity—Jews as well as Gentiles—are sinners and need to be saved. Second, since there is only **one God,** He must be God to all people. Third, God has provided one way of salvation and that is **through faith.**

Acts 15 records a crucial meeting of the leaders in the early churches. The issue was whether Gentile believers had to be circumcised and keep the Jewish law to be saved. Peter was one of the leaders who spoke out for the position of Paul. Peter made an important point when he said, "We believe that through the grace of the Lord Jesus Christ we shall be saved, even as they" (v. 11). In other words, Peter agreed with Paul that Gentile believers are saved by grace through faith in Jesus Christ. But he also stressed that this is the only way of salvation for Jews as well as Gentiles.

What are the lasting lessons in verses 29-30?

1. Faith in one God calls for Him to be the God of all people.

2. Jews, as well as Gentiles, can be saved only by grace through faith.

❖ *Spiritual Transformations*

The Bible study shows that all people stand before God without excuse for their sins and all deserve condemnation. No one can be declared righteous based on keeping the law, for all have sinned. But the Scriptures tell of the saving righteousness of God. This saving righteousness is available to those who have faith in Jesus Christ. God offers to declare sinners righteous through faith based on His grace. Thus salvation is the free gift of God to sinners, but this free gift cost the life of the Son of God. God set forth His Son as the propitiation for human sin. In Jesus' death the love and wrath of God came together. Because of Jesus' death for sinners, no one can charge that God is unjust; and because Jesus' death makes salvation possible, God is both just and the justifier of those who believe. This excludes human boasting, but calls for praise to God. This is the one way of salvation offered by the one God of all people.

What does this Bible lesson say to people who trust their own goodness as their hope for entering heaven? _____

_____

What would you say to someone who held this delusion? _____

_____

What does this passage say about how to be declared righteous by God? _____

How would you present this good news to someone who is lost? (See the inside front cover for more help in how to be saved.) _____

_____

If God has not declared you righteous, will you trust Him now? __

_____

Prayer of Commitment: Merciful God, I realize that I am a sinner and that Jesus died for my sin. Save me from my sin, accept me, although I am unacceptable. I am trusting Your mercy and love, not my own goodness. Amen.

[1]Mounce, "Romans," NAC, 110, note 180.
[2]Douglas J. Moo, *The Epistle to the Romans*, in The New International Commentary on the New Testament [Grand Rapids: William B. Eerdmans Publishing Company, 1996], 205.

SALVATION MEANS A NEW LIFE

Background Passage: Romans 5:1-21
Focal Passage: Romans 5:1-11,18-21
Key Verse: Romans 5:1

❖ *Significance of the Lesson*

• The *Theme* of this lesson is that faith in Jesus results in a new life.

• The *Life Question* this lesson seeks to address is, How am I different now that I'm saved?

• The *Biblical Truth* is that people who put their faith in Jesus Christ experience new life.

• The *Life Impact* is that you understand and enjoy your new life in Christ.

Does Jesus Make a Difference?

In a secular worldview, people question whether Christ makes any difference in the lives of those who follow Him. As evidence they point to the lives of professing Christians who seem no different than non-Christians. Some conclude that if any difference exists at all, it is defined in avoiding certain activities, abiding by rigid rules, doing good deeds, possessing certain subjective feelings, or assuming you'll go to heaven when you die.

The biblical worldview affirms that Jesus makes all the difference in people's lives. The new life in Christ satisfies the deepest human needs for life, love, hope, joy, and peace. Christians know these are things all people seek in their own ways but that they are found only in Christ.

Word Study: *peace with God*

Eirene is the Greek word for **peace**. The Greeks used it much as we use our word *peace.* Often the word is applied to cessation of hostilities or to inner peace of mind. In the New Testament the meaning of *eirene* is based on the use of the word in the Greek translation of the Old Testament, where it translates the rich Hebrew word *shalom*. This word refers to a person's total well being and to society's well being under God. Thus **peace** in the New Testament carries the same rich meaning as *shalom* in the Old Testament.

Notice that Romans 5:1 refers to **peace with God.** This is not the same as inner peace of mind and spirit, called "the peace of God" in Philippians 4:7. Nor is it the same as the peace among believers that Jesus brings (Eph. 2:14). However, these other expressions of peace grow out of peace with God. **Peace with God** in Romans 5:1 refers to a fruit of justification. It is the state of being reconciled to God.

❖ *Search the Scriptures*

Because of being justified through faith, believers have peace with God, live by grace, and hope for the glory of God. Christians can rejoice in sufferings because God works for good to produce transformed lives. God's love is the source of the life in Christ. The Spirit pours out love in our hearts. God's love was revealed in the death of Christ for the ungodly. If God died for us and reconciled us while we were sinners, we can be confident of His final salvation. As one man brought sin and death into the world, so Jesus Christ brought salvation and eternal life.

The Focal Passage Outline answers the Life Question, How am I different now that I'm saved? The outline lists five qualities of the new life in Christ.

Peace (Rom. 5:1-2)

How does being reconciled result in a new life for believers? Why is **peace with God** *the foundation for all true peace? What is the basis for our* **hope** *of new standing with God? What is the goal of Christian hope?*

Verses 1-2: Therefore being justified by faith, we have peace with God through our Lord Jesus Christ: ²by whom also we have access by faith into this grace wherein we stand, and rejoice in hope of the glory of God.

Therefore points back to Paul's explanation of justification through faith in Romans 3:21–4:25. This experience within itself leaves us standing before the bar of divine justice pardoned, but this is only the beginning of a new life in Christ. We are saved from something, but we are also saved for something. The unexpressed question that Paul begins to answer seems to be this: "So believers have been justified by faith. What now?"

Peace with God is one fruit of being justified. As noted in the "Word Study," this is the basis for all kinds of peace. **Peace with God,** for example, is the basis for the "peace of God" that passes human understanding (Phil. 4:7), and it is the basis for peace among believers (Eph. 2:14). Many people are looking elsewhere for peace of mind and for peace among nations, within nations, in communities, and in families. Ultimately, these must be based on peace with God. This is another way of describing what is in Romans 5:9-11, where Paul told how sinners as enemies of God are reconciled to God in Christ. **Peace with God** is the state of being reconciled to God. It assumes an ongoing relationship with the Lord, not just a one-time transaction.

All of this is possible only **through our Lord Jesus Christ.** It is through Him that we come into a new standing or relationship with God. The Greek word translated **access** can be translated "introduction" (NASB). Jesus has brought us into the presence of God and provides continuing access to Him. This is because God revealed in Christ that His is a throne of grace, to which we come to receive mercy and grace to help in time of need (Heb. 4:16). Our relationship with God is **grace** from beginning to end. Some people think that we are saved by grace and kept by works, but we are saved by grace and kept by grace.

Paul turned from past and present experiences of believers to look toward the future. **Hope** is the forward look of faith. The goal of this hope is **the glory of God.** "The glory of God is the end for which he created mankind, and it is through the redemptive work of Christ that this end will be achieved."[1]

What lasting lessons are in verses 1-2?

1. Being justified is the beginning, not the end, of a new life.

2. Peace with God is the basis for all kinds of peace.

3. Through Jesus Christ we have new standing with God based on His grace.

4. Christian hope focuses on the glory of God.

Hope (Rom. 5:3-4)

How can believers rejoice in suffering? How does God work for good in difficult circumstances? How is Christian hope different from secular hopes?

Verses 3-4: And not only so, but we glory in tribulations also: knowing that tribulation worketh patience; [4]and patience, experience; and experience, hope.

Rejoice and **glory** in verses 2 and 3 translate the same Greek word. This is not the usual word for "rejoice" (which is *chairo*; see Phil. 4:4). This word is translated "boasting" in 3:27. It can mean "boast," "exult," "glory," or "rejoice." When it refers to what we do about ourselves, it is bragging or boasting. When used of God, it is exulting or rejoicing. It combines elements of confidence and joy.

Both of these Greek words are used in the New Testament to describe the amazing teaching that Christians can **glory in tribulations** or "rejoice in our sufferings" (NIV). James 1:2 says to "consider it pure joy, my brothers, whenever you face trials of many kinds" (NIV; see also vv. 3-4). First Peter 1:6-7 is a similar statement. All three writers no doubt were reflecting the teaching of the Lord Jesus, when He said of the blessedness of those who are persecuted for the sake of the kingdom of heaven, "Rejoice, and be exceeding glad: for great is your reward in heaven" (Matt. 5:12). The word for **tribulations** means to live under the pressure of troubles. Some Bible students think that Paul had in mind only persecutions for the cause of Christ. More likely, he was referring to all kinds of sufferings and troubles.

The happiness pictured in verses 3-4 is totally incomprehensible by secular standards. Most people think that happiness is dependent on outward circumstances. Therefore, they seek to manipulate or manage circumstances in their pursuit of happiness. Some resort to the kind of pleasures that are morally and spiritually destructive. They do not know the secret that we need to share with them. True joy is found only in Christ. If we are right with Him, joy will be one of the fruits.

How can believers rejoice in suffering? Jesus and Peter spoke of the rewards of heaven. James and Paul spoke of the good results of enduring suffering with joy. The word for **patience** ("perseverance," NIV) means "to bear up under." When believers rejoice in troubles, they develop greater endurance. This in turn produces **experience.** The word means that which has been tested and passed the test. Thus it can be translated "proven character" (NASB). Tested character is more precious than gold refined in the fire (1 Pet. 1:7; see also Job 23:10).

Hope is a key word in this passage. It appears in verses 2,4,5. Christian hope, like Christian joy, is different from the hopes of secular people. Everyone has hopes in the sense of things they wish to be true. But biblical hope has a different goal and a different source. The goal is to glorify God. The source is the God of hope. He is the One who enables us to have the kind of faith, hope, and love that rejoices in the midst of troubles. He is the One who uses such endurance and tested character to further enhance our hope. Notice that this cycle begins and ends with hope. Romans 8:18-25 illustrates how hope enables us to endure and how enduring enhances hope.

What are the lasting truths in verses 3-4?

1. Christians can rejoice in times of trouble and suffering.

2. God is able to use this spirit to create and enhance endurance, character, and hope.

Love (Rom. 5:5-8)

Why does hope not disappoint us? What is the relationship between **hope** *and* **love***? What is the source of Christian love? Why is the love of Christ on the cross unique? How does the death of Christ reveal* **the love of God***?*

***Verse 5:* And hope maketh not ashamed; because the love of God is shed abroad in our hearts by the Holy Ghost which is given unto us.**

Maketh not ashamed can be translated "does not disappoint" (NKJV, NIV, NASB, NRSV, HCSB). This is true in this life, and it will be true when we stand before God in the final judgment. By contrast, the hopes of humanity constantly disappoint. The ancient Greeks said hope was a deceptive goddess luring people on to destruction with its false promises. But Christian hope makes no false promises.

In verse 5 Paul moved from **hope** to **love** in his presentation of the good news. Just as the God of hope is the source of Christian hope, so is the God of love the source of our love. This love is **shed abroad in our hearts by the Holy Ghost** [Spirit]. "God has poured out his love into our hearts by the Holy Spirit" (NIV). When Paul listed the fruit of the Spirit in Galatians 5:22-23, the first on his list was love.

Verses 6-8: **For when we were yet without strength, in due time Christ died for the ungodly. [7]For scarcely for a righteous man will one die: yet peradventure for a good man some would even dare to die. [8]But God commendeth his love toward us, in that, while we were yet sinners, Christ died for us.**

The death of Jesus was the highest expression of the love of God. This love is unique because Jesus died for us **while we were yet sinners.** In fact, **sinners** is only one of the words used to describe those for whom Christ died. We also were **without strength** and **ungodly.** In verse 10 we are described as **enemies.** Thus Christ died for people who were helpless and hostile.

Verse 7 seems to make a difference between **a righteous man** and **a good man.** Paul wrote that only rarely would someone give up his life for the first kind of person. This is an upright but uptight person. The other person is upright but has qualities of mercy and kindness. Some would be willing to die for such a person. Paul's point was that people are sometimes willing to lay down their lives for those whom they love and who love them. Many people have given their lives for their country and for their friends and family. But how many people are willing to give their lives for enemies, those who have hurt them and continue to be their enemies? This is what Jesus did when He died for those who were hostile to Him. This kind of self-sacrificial love for one's enemies is fully revealed at the cross.

Another interesting thing to notice is that Paul insisted in verse 8 that the cross reveals not only the love of Jesus but also the love of God: "God demonstrates his own love for us in this: While we were still sinners, Christ died for us" (NIV). We saw in 3:25-26 that the death of Christ revealed both the wrath and the love of God. The emphasis in 5:8 is on His love. "It would be easy to see the cross as demonstrating the indifference of God, a God who let the innocent Jesus be taken by wicked men, tortured, and crucified while he did nothing. And that would indeed be the case were it not that 'God was in Christ, reconciling the world to himself' (2 Cor. 5:19). Unless there is a sense in which the Father and Christ are one, it is not the love of God that the cross shows. But because Christ is one with God, Paul can speak of the cross as a demonstration of the love of God."[2]

What are the lasting lessons of verses 5-8?

1. Christian hope does not disappoint us.
2. God pours out His love in our hearts by the Holy Spirit.

3. Christ died for people who were helpless and hostile.
4. God reveals His love in the death of His Son.

Reconciliation (Rom. 5:9-11)

*From what area of life is the word **reconciled** taken? What is the cost of reconciliation? How do these verses teach the doctrine of security of believers? In what sense are we **saved by his life**?*

Verses 9-11: Much more then, being now justified by his blood, we shall be saved from wrath through him. [10]For if, when we were enemies, we were reconciled to God by the death of his Son, much more, being reconciled, we shall be saved by his life. [11]And not only so, but we also joy in God through our Lord Jesus Christ, by whom we have now received the atonement.

The Word of God presents its message of salvation using a variety of images from different areas of daily life. For the first time in Romans, Paul introduced another way to describe salvation. He wrote of being **reconciled to God.** We have noted that the language of *justification* came from the court of law, the language of *redemption* came from the slave market, and the language of *propitiation* came from the sacrificial altar. The language of *reconciliation* came from an area about which all of us know something. It came from the area of human relations. We know what it means to be estranged or alienated from someone and then to be reconciled to each other. This is the reality enacted on the larger screen of our relations with God.

To begin with, **we were enemies.** Because of human sin, people had alienated themselves from God. They turned their backs on Him and did things that were opposed to Him. They were at war with God. The alienation extended to God's relation with sinful humanity. Sin separates from God for two reasons: Sinners turn from God in rebellion, and a holy God is offended by their evil and ungodliness. A state of war existed between humans and God.

If a human case of estrangement is to be resolved, one of the parties must take the initiative in seeking to bring about reconciliation. In the Bible, God Himself is always the One who takes the initiative to reconcile sinful human beings who are in rebellion with Him. Just as in human reconciliation, so in the divine. God had to absorb the hurt and injury of the strife in order to forgive and offer a new relationship. God did this at Calvary—**We were reconciled to God by the death of**

his Son. Reconciliation, like the other ways of describing salvation, is made possible by the death of **Jesus Christ,** God's **Son.**

Reconciliation leads to a new relation with God. Justification leaves us pardoned at the bar of divine judgment. Reconciliation includes our coming into the arms of God as His children.

Paul's point in verses 9-11 was to provide assurance of our acceptance by God and of our future with Him. Notice that both verses 9 and 10 refer to salvation in the future. This is a strong passage supporting security of believers. Paul used a **much more** argument in verses 9 and 10. He began with the fact that we have been **justified by his blood.** Because this is true, Paul reasoned, **we shall be saved from wrath through him.** If God sent His Son to die in order to declare believers right with Him, He will surely save them from future wrath.

Verse 10 is even more striking. **We were enemies,** and God sent His Son to die for us and then to reconcile us to Himself. Because of this, we can be sure that **we shall be saved by his life.** In what sense are we **saved by his life**? This reminds us that the One who died for our sins is alive and continues His work within us by His Spirit. He also is the living intercessor for us (Heb. 7:25). We have been, are being, and **shall be saved** by God through the crucified, risen Lord. Another way to put it is this: We know that we shall be saved because we were saved from sin's penalty when we trusted Christ and we are being saved from sin's power by the Spirit's power. All phases of salvation are based on the grace of God, not on our actions. If salvation depended on us, none of us could have any assurance. But because all phases are based on the grace of God, we can have assurance. This assurance is based on Christ's death for us while we were enemies, God's search for us while we were fleeing from Him, and His forgiveness and reconciliation when He found us.

Verse 11 again uses the word for **joy** or rejoice: "Not only is this so, but we also rejoice in God through our Lord Jesus Christ, through whom we have now received reconciliation" (NIV). The last word in verse 11, which the *New International Version* renders "reconciliation," is translated **atonement** in the *King James Version*. **Atonement** is used to refer to "at-one-ment," an old way of describing reconciliation.

What are the lasting truths in verses 9-11?

1. Believers can be sure that they shall be saved from God's wrath.

2. The basis for this assurance is the death of Christ and our experience of being reconciled to God.

3. The biblical doctrine of reconciliation is taken from the area of personal relations.

Eternal Life (Rom. 5:18-21)

*How did Paul contrast the legacies of Adam and Christ? How are we to take the use of the words **all** and **many**? In what sense are people **made sinners**? What effect did the law have? If sin causes **grace** to **abound,** why not continue in sin, that grace may abound? Why is Christ the only source of **life**?*

Verses 18-19: Therefore as by the offense of one judgment came upon all men to condemnation; even so by the righteousness of one the free gift came upon all men unto justification of life. [19]For as by one man's disobedience many were made sinners, so by the obedience of one shall many be made righteous.

Romans 5:12-21 deals with the contrasting results of the sin of Adam and the salvation in Jesus Christ. These verses deal with the two major themes that Paul had dealt with to this point in his letter. Romans 1:18–3:20 emphasizes that all have sinned. Romans 3:21–5:11 stresses that sinners can be justified by faith only in Jesus Christ. Paul introduced this section of contrasts in verse 12—"Therefore, just as sin entered the world through one man, and death through sin, and in this way death came to all men, because all sinned" (NIV)—but then he digressed. This is why the *King James Version* places verses 13-17 in parentheses, because Paul interrupted his argument from verse 12 and does not resume it until verses 18-21.

Verses 18-19 are parallel in meaning, although different words are used to make the same point. In each verse Paul contrasted the actions, results, and recipients of what Adam did with what Christ did.

Verse 18:

Actor	Actions	Results	Recipients
Adam	**offense**	**condemnation**	**all**
Christ	**righteousness**	**justification of life**	**all**

Verse 19:

Adam	**disobedience**	**made sinners**	**many**
Christ	**obedience**	**made righteous**	**many**

Adam's "transgression" (NASB) brought the judgment of death to all. Christ's act of righteousness at the cross led to being declared right with God through faith in Christ. **Righteousness** in verse 18 is *dikaiomatos,* "act of righteousness," referring to Christ's death on the cross. **Justification of life** is clearer as "justification that brings life" (NIV). One transgression led **all** to be condemned. One act of righteousness opened the opportunity for **all** to believe and be saved.

We need to be careful about how we understand **all** when it refers to the life that comes from justification in verse 18. Some people refer to this verse as evidence that Paul taught that all would be saved. "Paul did not intend to imply that the result of Christ's atoning work automatically provided justification for all regardless of their willingness to accept it. Universal salvation is not taught in this text."[3]

Adam's **disobedience** resulted in **many** being **made sinners,** and Christ's **obedience** to the will of God resulted in **many** being **made righteous.** In verse 19 the word **many** with reference to the results of Adam's sin needs to be understood as "all" based on 3:23 and 5:12. In what sense did Adam's sin cause all to be **made sinners**? This is the key question debated by those who have studied Romans 5:12-21 over the centuries. In general, there are three basic views. Some people believe that each human being inherits the guilt of sin from birth. Others stress that although we inherit a sinful world, each person freely chooses sin when old enough to do so. A third view holds that we inherit a sinful environment and a sinful nature, but we are not held accountable for our actions until we make the decision to sin. This is the view in *The Baptist Faith and Message,* Article III, "Man." One sure fact is that all the descendants of Adam (except Jesus) have sinned. Thus Adam's legacy to the world was sin and death. Christ's legacy is salvation and life.

***Verses 20-21:* Moreover the law entered, that the offense might abound. But where sin abounded, grace did much more abound: ²¹that as sin hath reigned unto death, even so might grace reign through righteousness unto eternal life by Jesus Christ our Lord.**

Verse 20 brings in the issue of **the law.** Between Adam and Christ was the giving of the law. Here as elsewhere, Paul maintained that the law does not save but shows us our sins. The law caused **sin** to **abound** ("increase," NIV). But this was offset by the **grace** of God, which "increased all the more" (NIV). Romans 6:1-4 shows how some people tried to use this teaching as an excuse to sin more in order that more of God's grace could be revealed. Paul condemned such twisted thinking.

Verse 21 is a summary verse. Since the time of Adam, **sin hath reigned unto death.** By contrast, in Jesus Christ, **grace** reigns **through righteousness unto eternal life.** One of the precious results of being justified through Jesus Christ by the grace of God is the life we have in Jesus Christ. He is "the bread of life" (John 6:35), "the resurrection, and the life" (11:25-26), and "the way, the truth, and the life" (14:6). The word **life** tends to be associated with Jesus Christ. He came that we might have life and that we might have it abundantly (10:10). He came that we might have the gift of **eternal life** (3:15; 10:28; 17:2).

What are the lasting lessons in verses 18-21?

1. Christ came to reverse the rule of sin and death begun by Adam.

2. All have sinned and face condemnation, but Jesus offers eternal life to those who believe in Him.

❖ *Spiritual Transformations*

The fruit of being justified by grace through faith includes peace with God, hope that does not disappoint, love from God through the cross, reconciliation from being enemies with God, and life that is abundant and eternal.

What evidences does your life show of the reality of your salvation?

_____

What is the fruit of the new life in your own experience? _____

_____

How does peace with God form the basis of inner peace and peaceful relationships? _____

*How does your hope differ from the hopes of nonbelievers?*_____

_____

How well are you able to rejoice in troubles? _____

How much has the love of God been poured out in your life? _____

_____

How confident are you of eternal life in Jesus Christ? _____

Prayer of Commitment: Lord, create in me the fruit of salvation: life, love, hope, joy, peace, and reconciliation. Amen.

[1]F. F. Bruce, *The Epistle of Paul to the Romans*, rev. ed., in the Tyndale New Testament Commentaries [Grand Rapids: William B. Eerdmans Publishing Company, 1985], 114.

[2]Morris, *The Epistle to the Romans*, 224.

[3]Mounce, "Romans," NAC, 144.

SALVATION BEGINS A LIFE OF OBEDIENCE

Background Passage: Romans 6:1-23
Focal Passage: Romans 6:12-23
Key Verse: Romans 6:22

❖ *Significance of the Lesson*

- The *Theme* of this lesson is that salvation begins a life of obedience.
- The *Life Question* this lesson seeks to address is, What should I do now that I'm saved?
- The *Biblical Truth* is that people who receive salvation are freed from sin to obey God.
- The *Life Impact* is to help you live in obedience to God.

Freedom and Obedience

In the secular worldview life can be compartmentalized. Religious practices and sinful ways can peacefully coexist in a person's life. Some people who embrace religion want to continue living sinful lifestyles. Many Christians have never grown in holiness beyond their conversion or even consider that they need to do so.

In the biblical worldview believers have been set free from sin's penalty and are being set free from its power. They are to choose daily to say no to sin and to yield themselves to God. They believe that being saved is the beginning, not the end, of the Christian life.

Word Study: *yield*

The Greek verb translated **yield** in the *King James Version* appears several times in Romans 6:12-23. Most other translations use "offer" (NIV, HCSB) or "present" (NASB, NRSV, NKJV). The word has the basic meaning of "place beside." It was used at times of presenting something as a sacrifice (12:1). At other times it was used to mean "make yourself available to someone" (Matt. 26:53). In our Focal Passage it is parallel in meaning to "obey."

❖ *Search the Scriptures*

In these verses Paul was dealing with a common misconception of the Christian life—that being saved is the end, not the beginning, of life in Christ. Christians are to present themselves to God for righteous living. They are to be slaves of the Lord, not slaves of sin. People show their real master by whom they obey. Slavery to sin leads to death, but slavery to God leads to eternal life.

Call to Obedience (Rom. 6:12-14)

How do these verses relate to Romans 6:1-11? Since believers have been saved from sin, why did Paul warn them about letting sin rule over them? In verse 13, to what two ways can people give themselves? What does it mean to live not under the law, but under grace?

Verses 12-14: Let not sin therefore reign in your mortal body, that ye should obey it in the lusts thereof. [13]Neither yield ye your members as instruments of unrighteousness unto sin: but yield yourselves unto God, as those that are alive from the dead, and your members as instruments of righteousness unto God. [14]For sin shall not have dominion over you: for ye are not under the law, but under grace.

Chapter 6 begins with Paul's insistence that salvation by grace does not encourage sin. He stressed how believers have died to sin by Christ's death and how they have been raised to a new life by His resurrection from the dead. True believers have been set free from sin and death through Jesus Christ, and their lives show it.

Therefore points back to verses 1-11 and makes practical applications for what this means in how believers live. Although believers have been saved from sin's penalty and have the presence of the crucified, risen Lord within them, each still has a **mortal body** that is subject to temptations of sinful **lusts.** The word for **lusts** means "desires" (HCSB) and can refer to good or bad desires. Here they are "evil desires," as the *New International Version* makes clear. The evil desires often are lusts for sensual sins, but some evil desires are envy, covetousness, and selfish ambition. As long as we are in a mortal body (one subject to death), such temptations will continue. Paul's warning was not to let them **reign** in our lives. The danger sign of such an evil reign is obeying the call of the lower nature. **Obey** is used in these verses of obedience to sin and of obedience to God. The Greek word has the idea of hearing and heeding.

Verse 13 describes two different ways and exhorts believers to place themselves at the disposal of one but not of the other. **Members** refers to "parts" of the body without specifying specific parts. The idea is not to present "any parts" (HCSB) **as instruments of unrighteousness. Instruments** is a word that at times refers to "weapons" (HCSB). Paul warned believers not to allow any part of themselves to become a weapon of wickedness that the enemy could use against the work of Christ.

The positive counterpart of this warning uses some of the same words, but the key words are different: "Offer yourselves to God, and all the parts of yourselves to God as weapons for righteousness" (HCSB). Words in common in the two halves of the verse are **yield, members,** and **instruments.** However, instead of yielding **unto sin,** believers must yield themselves **unto God.** Instead of **instruments of unrighteousness,** believers yield themselves as **instruments of righteousness.**

Righteousness is the word Paul used earlier in Romans of God's righteousness and of being declared righteous by God's grace through faith. Here Paul was moving beyond justification to sanctification. God declares us righteous when we come to Him in faith. Then the Spirit of the crucified, risen Lord begins to transform our lives into His image. This includes a life of righteousness. This process of sanctification is no more a human work than justification. Both are possible only by the grace and power of God.

Alive from the dead shows that Paul continued the picture of death to sin and new life from verses 1-11. Verses 12-14 form a transition from this picture of the new life to the one in verses 15-23, which emphasizes freedom from sin. We see the new emphasis in words such as **reign** and **have dominion. Reign** is related to the word for "king." **Have dominion** is related to the word for "master" or "lord." In this context, Paul had in mind the master of slaves who obey without question.

Paul based this appeal on the fact that Christians are **not under the law, but under grace. Under** implies being subject to some king or lord. Paul dealt with the issue of the law in Romans. He made clear that keeping the works of the law could save no one. He taught that the law is good within itself, but that the law condemns the sinners who transgress it (which is everyone). The law condemns sinners to death. Thus Paul wrote of the need to be set free from sin, death, and the law. We no longer live under the condemnation of the law, but under the reign of the God of grace.

What are the lasting lessons in verses 12-14?

1. Believers should not allow sin to control their lives by yielding to sinful desires.

2. Rather than placing ourselves at the disposal of sin, we should place ourselves totally at the disposal of God.

3. Living under the law is condemnation; living under grace is salvation.

Principle of Obedience (Rom. 6:15-16)

How is verse 15 both similar to and different from verse 1? Why is it important to recognize that Paul was writing about slaves, not hired servants? Why are we free to choose but not free not to choose? Why do people want freedom but not obedience?

Verses 15-16: **What then? shall we sin, because we are not under the law, but under grace? God forbid.** **¹⁶Know ye not, that to whom ye yield yourselves servants to obey, his servants ye are to whom ye obey; whether of sin unto death, or of obedience unto righteousness?**

Verse 1 and verse 15 both contain quotes from Paul's critics. In 6:1 the critics were responding to what Paul wrote in 5:21 about grace abounding where sin most abounded. His critics asked if they should not sin more in order to allow grace to flourish. In 6:15 Paul had just written about living under grace, not law. Thus his critics asked, **Shall we sin, because we are not under the law, but under grace?** In both cases, Paul gave the same strong negative response. **God forbid** translates *me genoito.* This was a strong way for denying the truth of something. It can be translated in many ways: "Certainly not!" (NKJV, CEV), "By no means!" (NIV, NRSV), "May it never be!" (NASB), "Of course not!" (REB, NEB), and "Absolutely not!" (HCSB).

What was Paul's purpose in making this point in a letter to believers? One purpose no doubt was to help them answer the critics of Paul's gospel of grace. Another purpose probably was to challenge Roman believers who thought that since they had been saved by grace, God would not be concerned about an occasional sin. Baptists disagree with those groups who believe that sinless perfection is possible in this life; however, sometimes we are too quick to condone our sins as normal for believers. Such an attitude is dangerous.

Verse 16 explains why Paul reacted so negatively. Paul pointed out that we are slaves of whatever master we obey. **Servants** translates *doulous,* the word for "slaves" (NIV). Paul was not writing about hired servants who had the freedom to leave if they chose to do so. He was writing about slaves as they were in the first century. Slaves had no choice except **to obey** their master. Whoever people obey is shown to be their master. In the moral and spiritual realm, each person is either a slave of God or a slave of sin. Each of us chooses our master, but no one can choose not to have a master.

Most secular people object to two ideas in verse 16. On the one hand, they deny that sinners are slaves of anyone. They claim to be free to live as they choose. Jesus taught that those who live in sin are slaves of sin (John 8:34). Sin becomes addictive and produces a plight from which we cannot set ourselves free. Deliverance must come from some power beyond ourselves. God sets us free from sin when we trust Jesus as Lord and Savior.

The other idea that many object to is the claim that each of us serves some master—either God or sin. Jesus said that no one can serve two masters and that we cannot serve God and mammon (Matt. 6:24). God made us free to choose, but He did not make us free not to choose. If we are not slaves of God, we are slaves of sin. No one has the freedom to do exactly as he or she pleases.

Which of these two words leaves you with the most positive inner feelings—*freedom* or *obedience?* Most of us feel more warm and positive about freedom. **Obedience** conjures up the ideas of authorities who expect us to do what they want, not what we want. What we fail to remember is that life under the reign of God is true life and joy. Being slaves **of sin** leads to **death.** Being slaves of God leads to **obedience unto righteousness.** "The freedom of the Christian is not freedom to do what one wants, but freedom to obey God—willingly, joyfully, naturally."[1] This is also the way of life.

Obedience is the noun form of the verb **obey.** Obeying God is the way to life and fulfillment. His restrictions and commands are for our good. He warns us of those things that lead to death. He commands those things that lead to life.

What are the lasting truths of verses 15-16?

1. Some people look for every possible excuse for living in sin.
2. All people are either slaves of sin or slaves of God.
3. We choose our masters, but we cannot choose not to choose.
4. Freedom to do as one pleases is a form of slavery.
5. Obedience to God brings life and fulfillment.

Statement on Obedience (Rom. 6:17-19)

*How does God's Word help Christians to be obedient? How does God set us free from slavery of sin? Why does sin go from bad to worse? What did Paul mean by **holiness**?*

Verses 17-19: **But God be thanked, that ye were the servants of sin, but ye have obeyed from the heart that form of doctrine which was delivered you. ¹⁸Being then made free from sin, ye became the servants of righteousness. ¹⁹I speak after the manner of men because of the infirmity of your flesh: for as ye have yielded your members servants to uncleanness and to iniquity unto iniquity; even so now yield your members servants to righteousness unto holiness.**

Paul **thanked** the Lord that the Roman believers were no longer slaves **of sin.** The secret was stated like this: **ye have obeyed from the heart that form of doctrine which was delivered you.** This translation emphasizes the power of their reception of the Christian teachings. Most translations write not of the doctrine being delivered to them but of them being delivered to the doctrine. For example, the *New International Version* reads: "You wholeheartedly obeyed the form of teaching to which you were entrusted." This unusual way of stating the truth stresses that this was the work of God, not something humans did.

Form of doctrine refers to the body of Christian truths that we today have in the New Testament. The Word of God is crucial in living a life of obedience to the Lord. The Bible has two main purposes: (1) to lead us to salvation and (2) to lead us to live the Christian life. Those who live in the Word lay their lives down alongside God's measuring stick for Christian belief, living, and service. We see the areas in which we fall short and with God's help seek to change those areas.

Paul clearly stated in verse 18 what he earlier had implied. Believers have been **made free from sin.** The picture here is of someone imprisoned in a situation from which he cannot set himself free. God in Christ paid the price for our liberation, and He comes to set free those who will follow Him to freedom. How sad that some people cling to their chains instead of finding freedom in Christ. Even sadder are those who having been set free return to some of their old chains.

In verse 18b Paul made explicit that when we come to the Lord, we come as His slaves ready to obey Him. This obedience to God and His will results in life and fulfillment. The test of true faith is obedience. Are you doing what the Lord wants you to do? Are you doing it willingly and joyfully?

Paul explained why he used such human examples as slavery and freedom to describe moral and spiritual realities. Humans can understand only what we have either observed or experienced. We know about human slavery and being set free from it. Thus Paul used an analogy that his readers would understand.

The last part of verse 19 is an amplified version of verse 13. Paul's point was that they once **yielded** themselves totally **to uncleanness and to iniquity unto iniquity** ("ever-increasing wickedness," NIV). Sin always goes from bad to worse. Instead, Paul exhorted them to **yield** their **members servants to righteousness unto holiness. Holiness** translates *hagiasmon*, which usually is translated "sanctification" (NASB, HCSB, NRSV). This word is from a whole family built on the same root. From this root we get the English words for "holy," "saints," "sanctify," "make holy." This is another word, like "obedience," that people do not react to positively. It is a noble word that speaks of our commitment to the Lord as seen in how we live. God has set apart every believer to be holy. **Holiness,** like the word **righteousness,** is similar in meaning to obedience. Righteousness and holiness are the fruit of obeying God.

For as and **even so now** are words at the beginning of the descriptions of the two ways. Paul called believers to obey God with the same diligence with which they once obeyed the ways of sin.

What are the lasting truths in verses 17-19?

1. Living by God's Word is crucial for Christians.
2. Believers have been set free from sin and have become slaves of God.
3. The chief demand of our Master is obedience.

Results of Obedience (Rom. 6:20-23)

What is the end result of being slaves of sin? What is the end result of being slaves of God?

Verses 20-23: **For when ye were the servants of sin, ye were free from righteousness. [21]What fruit had ye then in those things whereof ye are now ashamed? for the end of those things is death. [22]But now being made free from sin, and become servants to God, ye have your fruit unto holiness, and the end everlasting life. [23]For the wages of sin is death; but the gift of God is eternal life through Jesus Christ our Lord.**

Paul admitted that slavery under the control of sin made people **free from righteousness.** This is why many non-Christians do not follow Christ. They want to be free to continue their own sins and to be free from God's demands. They believe that becoming a Christian would require them to give up the things that bring them most pleasure in life. They fail to recognize the enslaving power of sin that eventually leads to **death.**

Christians rejoice that we are free from the tyranny of sin, which leads to **death.** As Christians, we view our old lives through totally different eyes. We **are now ashamed** of **things** that we once considered as priceless and necessary for us to enjoy life. Being obedient to God brings a totally new life and outlook (see Phil. 3:7-8).

The biggest difference between being a slave of sin and a slave of God is in the end results. Those who were **made free from sin** have become slaves of God. The **fruit** of this relationship is "sanctification—and the end is eternal life!" (HCSB).

Verse 23 is a good summary not only of Romans 6 but also of the Bible as a whole. The entire message is here in a nutshell. On the one hand, the Bible warns us that **the wages of sin is death. Wages** show that the punishment is earned and deserved for those who have lived in sin. **Death** is more than physical death; it is the second death of eternal separation from God. People must hear this negative message to see their need for the positive message. **Gift** reminds us that salvation is God's free gift based on His great love and grace. **Eternal life** begins with conversion and it never ends. Physical death is only a transition from life in Christ here to life in Christ forever hereafter.

What are the lasting truths in verses 20-23?

1. Those who reject Christ want to be free from God's commandments.
2. Christians are now ashamed of the things that they once treasured.
3. The end result of sin's slavery is eternal separation from God.
4. The end result of slavery to God is eternal life.

Hugo Culpepper was a Southern Baptist missionary who was taken prisoner by the Japanese during World War II. He spent over three years imprisoned in the Philippines. American forces liberated him and others in his prison on February 5, 1945. When he was asked to write of his experience of being liberated, here is part of what he wrote:

"It was like passing from death to life! Everything we did had flavor and deep meaning. . . . We began to live with enthusiasm and zeal. I came to understand as never before what it means to be 'saved!'

"First of all, I had a deep sense of appreciation for the privilege of being free and of living in the United States. I had experienced what it means to be crushed under the domination of forces beyond my control. I had been restored to freedom of thought and speech. I was free to take initiative, to make plans, and to work for their achievement. I had a sense of direction and purpose in life. I had the exhilarating experience of true self-expression for worthwhile activities. And with all of this, I had a deep feeling of gratitude for the gift of life.

"I also had a profound feeling of responsibility. . . . Because I had been saved by God's grace, I returned to try to live my life on a higher level, to live more dynamically in every way."[2]

After reading this moving testimony, note some points that fit parts of this lesson.

1. Sin enslaves people under conditions from which they cannot free themselves.

2. Deliverance comes from an outside source. By their own efforts, persons cannot deliver themselves from slavery to sin.

3. Salvation brings new joy.

4. Salvation leads to a new sense of gratitude for the gift of life.

5. The gift of life leads to a new sense of responsibility.

❖ Spiritual Transformations

Paul called on the Roman Christians to yield to God and His way and to resist temptations to sinful desires. He warned that sin leads to slavery. Obeying God also involves yielding to His lordship. Paul told them that God's control of their lives brings joy, fulfillment, and eternal life but that slavery to sin leads to eternal separation from God.

Check each of the following that reflects your attitude or actions:

_____ *Being saved is only the beginning of the Christian life.*

_____ *I guard against yielding to temptations to sinful desires.*

_____ *I obey God's will in His Word and as His Spirit leads.*

_____ *I testify that obedience to God brings joy and fulfillment.*

How do you intend to improve your obedience to God? _____
_____

Prayer of Commitment: Dear Lord, help me to obey You willingly, joyfully, and continually. Amen.

[1]Moo, *The Epistle to the Romans*, 399.

[2]Hugo Culpepper, "What It Means to Be Saved," *Adult Bible Teaching Guide*, January, February, March 1970, 47-48.